THE PITFALL OF TRUTH

Holy War, Its Rationale And Folly

THE
PITFALL
OF TRUTH

Holy War, Its Rationale And Folly

Vel Nirtist

OVERVIEW BOOKS

NEW YORK

Cataloging Data

Nirtist, Vel (pseud.)
The Pitfall of Truth: Holy War, its Rationale and Folly/by Vel Nirtist.
    p.   cm.
Includes bibliographical references and index.
ISBN 1-933020-18-0
1. Current issues - Terrorism. 2. Philosophy - Epistemology.
3. Religion - Comparative religion. 4. Religion - Theology.
5. History - Wars of religion. 6. Spirituality.

Overview Books, P. O. Box 290-098
Brooklyn NY 11229-0098

www.overviewbooks.com

1 2 3 4 5 6 7 8 9 0

Printed and made in the USA

CONTENTS

INTRODUCTION

Centuries ago, a curious custom existed in Russia. When asking for a favor, a petitioner knelt in front of his superior and beat the floor with the forehead to show his total loyalty that merited the looked-for reward. Needless to say, this was a very delicate procedure, requiring much skill in performance: excessive show of zeal in petitioning could be very detrimental to health.

Russians were quick to generalize on that lesson and used it as a focal point of a proverb that advises moderation in every – even the most critical – activity. "Make a fool pray to God, and he'll break his head" is still current among the Russians. Though in itself a great example of condensed wisdom of the simple folk, this proverb is slightly inaccurate. As history teaches us, it is usually someone else's head that gets broken in a religious fool's holy zeal.

Religion may indeed be able to relieve some of the pain accompanying our existence, but it is a medicine with dreadful side effects – as the events of September 11th, 2001, made clear yet again. Sincere piety so often goes hand-in-hand with hatred and violence that they frequently seem to be the two sides of the same coin. This paradox is well worthy of examination; yet either out of misguided political correctness or because the subject of religion is so murky, little of substance has been said about the role of religion in religious violence. Instead, terror-ism is being blamed on ignorance, poverty, thirst for power, political grievances, "perversion of religion," "evil" – in other words, anything and everything other than religion.

The present writer sees no point in blaming external fac-tors, be they social, economic, political or metaphysical. In-stead, he focuses on the phenomenon of religion itself, and shows how it affects the minds to foster violence that threat-ens the very foundations of the free world.

CHAPTER 1

A GLANCE
AT HISTORY

A Bird's Eye View

A brief tour of history will amply demonstrate the fact that religion is indeed often accompanied by violence. Though our generation had been awoken to the fact of religious violence by the terrible events of September 11th, 2001, similar catastrophes have happened throughout human history. Let us take a bird's eye view; let us follow the trail of the faithful. Proceeding in a broadly chronological order, we will start with the Jews of the Old Testament and move on to the Christians adhering to the New; farther on, to Moslems heeding the message of Mohammed, that "Seal of the Prophets;" and, finally, to young idealists who, inspired by great discoveries of laws that presumably move humankind, have recently endeavored to build a couple of ultimately just societies, one enforcing the rights of oppressed productive workers, the other one populated by the best and the purest among humanity.

THE JEWS

Abraham's Obedience

The first great believer, of whom we have a good deal of information, is Abraham. Jews, Christians, and Moslems all see in him their greatest paragon of faith. His reputation in this respect is most solid, and it is all the more instructive to examine the way in which he managed to earn it. Let us turn to the Bible to learn his story. Beloved by God, Abraham was ever obedient to Him. He left his native country to follow the call of God, Who led him thousands of miles away from his homeland, promising to make of him a father of a great people, in whom all the peoples of the world would be blessed. Abraham dwelt in the Promised land for many long years, until he become very old. He remained childless, but never doubted God's promise. His faith was rewarded. When Abraham was about one hundred years old (and his wife Sarah not much younger), they had a son, Isaac. Then God decided to test Abraham's faith. He ordered Abraham to sacrifice Isaac to Him. To please God, Abraham did indeed pull the knife on his son and surely would have killed him, but for a last-minute divine intervention.

MOSES' ZEAL

Abraham was a man of strong faith, and so were a great many of his followers. As we follow the biblical narrative of the history of the nascent Jewish people, we read how the family of Abraham's grandson Jacob moves in order to dwell in Egypt, prospering and multiplying, only to become enslaved by the Egyptians, and be led out of Egypt by the great prophet Moses. After the exodus from Egypt, God calls Moses to mount Sinai to confirm the covenant between God and the Jews, as was promised to Abraham, and to instruct Moses in the Law that the Jews should follow, to be worthy of a covenant with the Holy One. This meeting between God and Moses turns out to be rather lengthy. Their conversation runs for forty days, non-stop, and the gathered Jews, waiting at the foot of the mountain get a bit impatient. For even with all of the miracles they have witnessed since the beginning of their exodus, not all have a strong faith. Some, forgetting that having no food nor drink for forty days is no big deal when in communion with God, start to suspect that Moses had met with an accident and left them to their own devices. Crude and uncouth in their theology and modes of worship, they collect all the precious metal they can get a hold of, and make a statue of a calf to worship. Warned by God of what was going on, Moses quickly came back and saw the outrage with his own eyes. They were incorrigible. Nothing but blood – preferably lots of it – could redeem his fellow Jews. "Then Moses stood at the gate of the camp, and said, Who is on the Lord's side? let him come unto me. And all the sons of Levi gathered themselves together unto him. And he said unto them, Thus saith the Lord God of Israel, put every man his sword by his side, and go in and out from gate to gate throughout the camp, and slay every man his brother, and every man his companion, and every man his neighbor. And the children of Levi did according to the word of Moses: and there fell of the people that day about three thousand men." The faith has triumphed once again.

SAUL'S FAILURE

Not that there was not an occasional snafu. As the Jews established themselves in the Promised land, they were beset by other peoples and tribes who harassed them a great deal. A tribe of Amalekites was particularly nasty to the Jews during their exodus from Egypt and later on. So God, speaking through prophet Samuel, ordered king Saul of Israel to utterly exterminate this hostile people. "Thus saith the Lord of hosts, I remember that which Amalek did to Israel, how he laid wait for him in the way, when he came up from Egypt. Now go and smite Amalek, and utterly destroy all that they have, and spare them not; but slay both man and woman, infant and suckling, ox and sheep, camel and ass." To our modern sensibilities the order may seem somewhat excessive, and we would expect Saul to be troubled with the command to kill babies. But genocide was a common practice in international relations of the time. Saul obeyed. He went to Amalekites' strongholds, proclaiming to them his intentions, and warned the friendly tribe of Kenites that lived among the enemy to get out of the doomed country. Once the Kenites were out of the way, Saul's army fell upon the enemy. None of the Amalekites was spared – neither man nor woman, neither infant nor suckling, in accordance with the word of the Command.

And yet, not every part of the divine command had been scrupulously fulfilled. The king's soldiers, while having no qualms with putting to sword the much-hated enemy and its offspring, were reluctant to destroy the good cattle that belonged to the Amalekites. To be sure, they had no impious hopes of personal lucre. On the contrary, they wanted to offer Amalekites' cattle as a sacrifice. (And, since part of sacrificial offering, according to the Law, was to be eaten, one suspects they were planning to have quite a party, too.) However it may have been, Samuel was divinely forewarned of what was going on, and was furious with such flagrant breach of the Command. The manifestly good intentions of the soldiers did not mollify him. Saul ought to have known better; he should not have allowed such outrage. "Hath the Lord as great delight in burned offerings and sacrifices, as in obeying the voice of the Lord?" he thundered at unfortunate Saul. "Behold, to obey is better than sacrifice, and to hearken than the fat of rams. For rebellion is as a sin of witchcraft, and stubbornness is as iniquity and idolatry. Because thou hast rejected the voice of the Lord, he hath also rejected thee from being king." Saul was never again able to regain Samuel's trust. Worse still, God turned away from Saul, too. Saul's end, though heroic, was pitiful. Deprived of God's help, Saul's army was defeated in the battle with Philistines, his sons fell in action, and Saul killed himself by falling on his own sword rather than be taken alive by the enemy. Were it not for his seemingly minor fault, he would have kept the favor of God and God's prophet till his dying days and would have left the throne of Israel to his heir. Saul allowed himself to be guided by his sensibilities rather than God's will, and the story of his failure and fall was a good lesson to the faithful, teaching them never to abate their zeal in executing divine commands. The best among them heeded this lesson and did not fail, as our excursion through history will continue to demonstrate.

RABBINICAL DISPUTES

To proceed with Jewish history, for many centuries Jews lived in the Promised land, first beating off their enemies, then quarreling among themselves to the point of letting their kingdom be split in two and be conquered by Assyria; they were exiled by Babylon, and then some of them came back to the Promised land. A temple was destroyed and rebuilt and spiritual guidance had moved from prophets to the rabbis. All this time, a far-off power was growing stronger and stronger, through the conquest of the neighboring lands and peoples. Among many other lands, Rome captured the Promised land, too. At about the time of Jesus, there was a good deal of debate among the rabbis on how to deal with Roman occupiers. A school of rabbinical law headed by Hillel tended to prefer just weathering the storm. Many in the school of Shammai, on the other hand, thought that the right way to deal with the crisis was to rise up in arms. Disciples of Shammai had strong faith in God's plans in this matter. Why even argue? The zealous disciples of the school of Shammai stood with swords and spears and "slew disciples of the School of Hillel." "And Eleazar went up accompanied by disciples, and they smote Elchanan [the high Priest] and cut him up into pieces." "That day they overfilled the measure," the rabbis of the later generation recollected. That day "was as grievous for Israel as the day on which they made the calf."

HASSIDIC SCHISM

Romans suppressed the rebellion and exiled the Jews, who have since been forced into outskirts of history and, until recently, been politically controlled and dominated by Christians and Moslems. Outside control, to which the Jews have been subjected ever since the loss of their statehood, was not conducive to internal religious strife. Yet, the strength of their faith occasionally continued to manifest itself. So it was in the case of a new religious movement called Chassidism, which started to spread among the Jews of Ukraine in the middle of the eighteenth century. Chassidism stressed an emotional, even ecstatic, involvement of the believer, in total contrast to the traditional Jewish approach based on coldly intellectual study of Talmud. Chassidic communities were led by charismatic leaders called rebbes, who were thought by their followers to possess miraculous powers. To traditional Jews all this was errant heresy, and they anathematized and proscribed the new sect, prohibiting the orthodox to marry them or to eat their food. That, of course, did not help much. On the contrary, the movement kept spreading. Then, a different way to stay the spread of heresy was found. Unable to resort to physical extermination of the heretics, the orthodox decided to ask the Christian authorities to take care of the subversive movement. Some Chassidic leaders were arrested and imprisoned, but eventually nothing came of the scheme. In our own time, as evidenced by reports that some ultra-orthodox in Israel are throwing stones at motorists who drive during the Sabbath, we may be sure that spirit of the faithful is alive and well. Assassination of the prime minister Rabin of Israel, who negotiated the release of some parts of the Promised land to the Palestinians, was also motivated by the purest religious sentiment.

CHRISTIANS

The history of Christianity abounds with acts of violence, too. It even offers a curious case of self-inflicted violence inspired by faith, perhaps one of only a few cases to occur before the Moslem suicide bombers. Discovering that sinful flesh distracted him from spiritual pursuits, Origen, one of the greatest fathers of the early church, was inspired by a line of God's word and "have made himself eunuch for the kingdom of heaven's sake," to change St. Matthew's inspirational phrase from plural into singular. But this act of willing self-mutilation was really an exception. In the mainstream – self-flagellation excepting – the believers demonstrated the strength of their faith through the violence vented on others.

SUFFERING AND TRIUMPH

Of course, Christians themselves suffered a lot before coming to a position of power and dominance. For three centuries after Jesus died on the cross and brought Salvation to his followers, Christianity was a despised and hated religion. By refusing to follow state-sanctioned religious rituals and to sacrifice to Roman gods, Christians were breaking Roman laws and customs and were often treated as criminals. They faced tidal waves of persecution. Thousands of early Christians were fed to wild animals in Roman circuses. But no amount of persecution could force them to waiver from the saving faith. However dangerous the times, Christians continued to spread the all-important news of salvation to their neighbors until, finally, even the Roman Emperor – Emperor Constantine – recognized the will of God and proclaimed Christianity the official religion of the Roman Empire. Christianity survived the period of hatred and persecution to become the dominant religion of Europe. Christians not only had nothing to fear, but they had all the encouragement and help from civil administrators they could wish for. And the Church itself became all-powerful by exercising the ultimate spiritual authority.

THE FIRST CRACKS

At this point in history, one could only expect arrival of the universal peace and bliss, but it was not to be. Keeping the faith strong proved a hard task. There were some who declined to follow God's word. To add insult to injury, the culprits were not so much the pagans but the professed Christians whose faith became corrupt. This was shockingly exemplified by the behavior of the Nubian churches, famous for their unswerving self-sacrifice in times of Roman persecution. Contrary to the articles of faith clearly expostulated to them, they denied authority to ministers who faltered and compromised themselves in the terrible times of Roman attacks on Christians. They held some other erroneous views; for example, they advocated adult baptism. In the early fourth century their opposition to certain appointments within the Church, on grounds of unworthiness of candidates, brought the Church to the brink of schism. The heretics, known as Donatists, proved extremely obstinate and would not recognize God's will when it was plainly shown to them. Their Christian brethren admonished them to abandon their erroneous ways, but admonition failed. Finally, the cele-

brated St. Augustin – the holy doctor of the church, the saintly
author of that great classic of Christian thought, the famous
"City of God," – was divinely inspired to find a better way to
enlighten the stubborn enemies of God. He taught the Donatists with the help of leaden whips; when they persisted, he
had them expelled and their property confiscated. This truly
inspired way of teaching God's will proved a total success. For
all the obstinacy of Nubian Donatists, the faith had triumphed
yet once again.

THE GREAT SCHISM

The faith stood unchallenged for a few centuries, then hit another snag. After the reign of Constantine, the Roman Empire
gradually disintegrated, splitting into two parts. The western,
Latin part was ruled out of Rome. The eastern part, or Byzantine Empire, was administered out of Constantinople, and
became the citadel of the Greek Orthodox church. Over time,
disagreements arose between the two centers of faith. In fact,
the dispute was over some important, if not vital, aspects of
Christianity. The Western Church proclaimed that the Holy
Spirit was proceeding from God the Son as well as from God
the Father; Constantinople did not think so and loudly objected. There was also much argument about God's will regarding
the proper form of divine service. Should unleavened bread
be used in the Eucharist? Should there be fasting on the Satur-
days during Lent? Should clergy be permitted to marry? Zeal
to implement God's will became so ardent that only a complete
break-up could solve the argument. In 1054 Constantinople
and Rome mutually excommunicated each other.

THE MOSLEM THREAT

Meanwhile, there emerged a threat to Christianity from without. For Christianity was not the only religion on the rise – some six centuries after Jesus had preached, another powerful and proselytizing religion arose: Islam. Its message was both simple and appealing, and it spread through the Middle East and Northern Africa with the speed of a whirlwind. Moslems established powerful states and developed sophisticated culture. And they were strong militarily. Pushing out of the center of the Arabian peninsula, they went on a relentless campaign of conquest, and within less than a century after Mohammed's death in 632, their empire covered half of the then-known world, from Spain through North Africa all the way to the border of India. They would have swamped Europe, too, but two defeats – one suffered at the hands of the army of Byzantine Emperor Leo III in 717, and another, in central France, from the forces led by Charles Martel in 732 – fixed the borders of their possessions in Europe along the southern border of France, and in Asia Minor, at the border with the Byzantine Empire. The Holy Land had been in possession of the Moslems since the seventh century. By the end of the eleventh century the pressure on the Christian states increased; Turks were in a position to attack Constantinople. At the same time, Europe was being torn apart by armed bickering between powerful barons, and the military power of Christian Europe, which could have been used to stem the advance of Islam and to uphold the Christian Faith, was being wasted in power struggles among the barons. Pope Urban II recognized the opportunity, and in November 1095, he preached a crusade for the liberation of Christian holy places from Moslem enemies of God. His appeal had the effect of a spark in a powder keg.

Liberation of Jerusalem

Christian Europe rose, almost to a man, to defend the faith. Though the initial assault by the first group of the faithful (who were disorganized poor peasants led by one Peter the Hermit) failed, and they all were killed by the Turks, success quickly followed. A strong and well-organized army had gathered one year after the Pope's appeal, and had crossed into Constantinople. The Byzantine forgot old disputes and did all they could to help in the great cause that inspired the Christendom. Crusaders were transported to Asia Minor by the Byzantine and, after a two-year-long campaign, managed to reach Jerusalem in 1099. The city was taken by storm, and its 10,000 Moslem and Jewish inhabitants were put to death.

Crusaders established the Kingdom of Jerusalem and for many years everything went well. But the political map of the Islamic world was gradually changing. Turks were becoming stronger and started to retake Crusaders' outposts in Asia Minor. The star of Saladin rose high, and in 1171 he took possession of Egypt. Shortly after, the King of Jerusalem died, and his death caused bitter struggles between the powerful barons of the kingdom and started armed strife between monastic military orders. It was almost a civil war. All portended ill for the Crusaders. In 1187, Jerusalem fell to Saladin.

Christian Europe was aghast at that disaster, but the Crusaders did not give up. Several unsuccessful attempts to recover Jerusalem followed, and finally Crusaders decided to take a more strategic approach and finish off the enemies of God once and for all. They planned to attack and capture what was then the heartland of Moslem power: Egypt. Military preparations went well, and the crusaders soon embarked the ships of Venice and sailed off to fight the enemies of God in Northeast Africa.

Byzantine Incident

But Providence had other plans.

In 1204 Venetian ships with Crusaders on board arrived at Constantinople, instead of Egypt. The cynics maintain that Venetian ship owners deliberately took a detour in a hope to incite the Crusaders' army against Constantinople, their major business competitor in the Mediterranean. Yet, this is not to be accepted as a dogma. Were not the Byzantine Greeks, though formally professing Christianity, in a manifest error? Had they not shown themselves hostile to the Church of Rome, this upholder of God's will? Would Christians have lost the Holy City of Jerusalem, had the Byzantine been loyal to Christ and faith? Didn't the Byzantine deserve a chastisement? Crusader's unintended arrival at the walls of Constantinople had every hallmark of divine will. The heretical city had to be chastised, so that Christendom could clean itself of all error before challenging the Moslem enemies of God, and obtain divine aid in the battle. Spirits of the Crusaders rose high; their hearts were beating fast. They could not even think of leaving the sins of false Byzantine unpunished. On April 12, 1204, Constantinople was attacked, taken, and sacked.

Albigensian Heresy

This incident gave the Pope an excellent idea for how to deal with certain dangerous enemies of God, who thrived right in the midst of Christian Europe, in Southern France, in what was then the county of Provence. In a way they were much more dangerous than the Moslems, for they masked themselves in the garb of Christianity and were better positioned to corrupt the hearts and poison the spirits of the faithful.

They were called Albigensians, and they advocated ideas that had nothing to do with the word of God. Largely owing their views to the gnostics of the early centuries of Christianity, the Albigensians took dualism of God and the Devil to its utmost logical conclusion, teaching that flesh (and all matter in general) had to do with the Devil, just as the Spirit was associated with God. Activities that indulged flesh, such as sex or fancy food, were anathema to them, and therefore they were ascetic to the utmost. Naturally, their abstemious way of life was perceived as holy, and because of that perceived holiness, the heretics commanded great respect, both among the common people and the higher-ups. That, of course, was highly conducive to the spread of the disease of heresy. The heretics were already found in the castles of powerful barons of Provence; they were held in awe by those in the highest echelons of local power. What more needs to be said? The head of state, Count Raimond VI of Toulouse was himself an Albigensian supporter. Not surprisingly, all protests by the pope, and all supplications to return to the path of faith were in vain. The deluded heretics were just too secure and felt very well-positioned to defy the power of Rome.

But faith was strong and it triumphed over Albigensean heresy. Four years after the sack of Constantinople, Pope Innocent III preached a crusade against the Albigensians. The success of the Crusaders against the bedarkened-by-the-Devil Provencal enemies of faith was beyond belief. The very first Provencal stronghold they attacked, a strongly fortified town called Beziers, fell to them within days, though the military commanders expected a prolonged siege, perhaps of several months. Great was the joy of the godly at such a certain and heartening sign of divine favor and approval; but that joy was marred by a practical problem. Only very few among the citizens were actual heretics to be eradicated; how were these

Devil-perverted monsters to be found among so many good Christians, who were as sincerely faithful as the Crusaders themselves? With so much country yet to be subdued, with so much heresy yet intact, the Crusaders wanted to maintain their momentum; ascertaining who was who among that city's population required a careful and prolonged investigation, for which they had no time to spare. Great as their difficulty was, the solution eventually was given to them by the spiritual leader of that crusade, Arnald-Amalric, abbot of Citeaux. He must have been as ingenious as he was full of pure faith, and his solution must have been divinely inspired indeed, since it was breathtakingly simple, exceptionally workable and, indeed, demonstrated the unfathomable depth of his faith. "Kill them all" – he suggested with a shrug of his shoulders – "God will look after His own." This most excellent and inspired advice was taken; the town's entire population was put to death. The rest of the Crusade went equally well. In June of 1210 the town of Minerve was captured, and a hundred and forty heretics were burned in one great fire. After the prolonged siege and capture of the supposedly impregnable mountainous fortress of Montsegur and the burning of two hundred Albigensian heretics inside, the triumph of the faithful over Albigensean heresy was complete. The Albigensian crusade was a success. The heresy was suppressed, the faith had triumphed.

PROPHYLACTIC MEASURES

But the faithful looked ahead. They were just too conscientious and scrupulous in defense of the faith to simply sit and glorify in their present success. They were contrite and self-critical and they were painfully aware that contamination of Provence by the accursed heretics was perhaps a result of their own fault. Something was very wrong with the way they were tending God's flock, or else the Devil would not have found a foothold in the South of France. In their heart of hearts they knew they had to change the way they went about their spiritual duties. They honestly searched their souls, and God inspired them with the answer. The heresy went undetected because there was too little supervision over the flock of the faithful. The regular parochial system did not allow for checking every word that was uttered, or for inquiring into every thought that crossed one's mind, and comparing these words and thoughts to the word of God. The supervision should have been much stricter, control ought to have been much tighter. If the proper supervisory structure had been in place, the thoughts placed into idle minds by the Devil would have been more easily detected and effectively fenced off. The heretical idea would have died, barren and powerless, with the one who first conceived it, well before it could have reached the ears and soiled godly simplicity of the innocent, or troubled the purity of mind of the faithful. An entirely new system of defense against the Devil cried to out be established – and it was. To defend innocent faith, the pope established the Holy Inquisition.

It is unnecessary to say much of this well-known institution that faithfully guarded the innocence of the faithful for six long centuries. This godly organization honestly earned its bread from a society, whose greatest treasure – its faith – it zealously guarded. No wonder the Holy Inquisition had been such a success. Its purposes were pure and worthy, and it was managed by the best and most able among the faithful. Only the most trusty among the believers were allowed to arrange twigs and wood for the Acts of Faith (which was a highly proper appellation for the solemn ritual of burning the accursed enemies of God at the stake.)

The immediate task set before that Holy organization was to complete the destruction of the benighted Albigensians and put a stop to further spread of their heresy. The first inquisitors performed that task nobly. No believer needed to fear the Albigensian disease: for one, not many survived who knew what it was all about; but also, too few were brave enough to allow it to be whispered in their ears, knowing full well the potential danger. The only bit of trouble was, that having extinguished the last remnants of Albigensian heresy, the Inquisitors did not have much to do. They would, of course, routinely perform their supervisory function. They would travel all over the district, whose population they were appointed to guard from the Devil's attacks on the purity of faith, and would preach the dangers of heresy to the local residents. They would tell them to confess the heresy within a two-week period of leniency, at their peril. Once in a while, the hidden heresy would be disclosed through the good offices of some pious, God-fearing local resident informing the inquisitor of suspicious activities. The inquisitor would than order the suspects arrested. He would present the accusations to them, not telling them, of course, the name of the informant in order to protect that godly man from possible revenge by the enemies of God. If they persisted in denying any wrongdoing, the inquisitor had the means to persuade them of the justice of the accusation. Having belatedly confessed under the hands of the torturer, the heretics would be burned at the stake, and their property seized from their heirs, to help the Church in strengthening the Faith. But such incidents did not happen too often; the fear of the Devil, the fear of departing from the path of faith, was well learned by the populace.

THE CLEANSING OF SPAIN

Such leisurely, routine pace was suddenly changed when an urgent appeal for help came out of Spain. After it was re-conquered from the Moslems in the fifteenth century, a considerable number of Jews in residence there were compelled to convert to Christianity. Those converts made brilliant careers in Spanish military, finance, medicine, and at the court. But strong doubts had ever been crossing the minds of their sovereigns, the Catholic King Ferdinand and Queen Isabella, about the sincerity of these new Christians. Though the converts diligently attended Church services and scrupulously performed all required Christian rituals, could it be that they still secretly clung to their old ways, which they seemed to have repudiated by undergoing Holy baptism? What if their meticulous observance was merely a mask hiding the unthinkably horrible betrayal of the faith? The terrible thought sat heavily on the hearts of the monarchs. God had entrusted them with both the temporal and the spiritual well-being of their subjects, and they wished to do their duty well. They were not going to betray the heavy trust that God put on them when He gave them the realm of Spain to rule. They did not wish to be accused at the Last Judgment of condoning spiritual double-dealing. The monarchs sought spiritual advice and assistance. To help the royal couple out of its doubt, the pope introduced Inquisition into Spain.

One of the strongest in faith in the whole realm of Spain, the confessor of their Catholic Majesties, the ascetic and incorruptible Tomas da Torquemada, was put in charge of purification of faith in 1483. The effect was striking. Sundays in every Spanish city suddenly became full of pageantry. Solemn processions of gaudily-dressed clergy and civic leaders could be seen moving across the city on the Lord's day, escorting those who had failed in their faith to their just punishment at the stake. Thousands were burned, strengthening the faith of millions, who gleefully watched them die. The experience thus gained and funds thus acquired were later used in eradicating

Protestants and other enemies of faith.

BIZARRE ASTRONOMY

Some errors did not directly collide with the articles of faith, yet were dangerously close to doing so. Such errors, though seemingly outside of the realm of spirit, also needed correction and were dutifully attended to by the Inquisition. Thus, a mid-sixteenth-century astronomer by the name of Copernicus had advanced a bizarre theory that the Earth was not the Center of the Universe but merely one of the planets moving around the Sun. This manifest error would have probably cost Copernicus his life, but the wily fellow died while his book was in the press, well before his error had been made public. Luckily, the new theory did but little damage, because the learned took it for a mere ingenious computational device, helping in finding out positions of the planets in the nightly sky, rather than for a statement of fact. But some sixty years later, an Italian astronomer named Galileo turned the new invention – telescope – to the heavens. While examining the phases of the planets, which this new instrument allowed one to see for the first time ever, he discovered strong evidence that the Earth indeed rotated around the Sun – and published his research. The church was alarmed. Earth not the Center of Creation? That made no sense, was totally deranged, dangerously wrong. Truth cried for intervention on its behalf. The Holy Inquisitors demanded an apology, and they won the battle for the Truth. In 1632 Galileo repudiated his error without having the Inquisition demonstrate the strength of its arguments.

WALDENCES AND HUSSITES

But for all its good work, the Holy Inquisition was only partially successful in its defense of faith. Some heretics dwelled in inaccessible mountains, and, for all the hard work of eradicating them, they survived still, though, of course, in much lesser numbers. Waldences, a heretical sect appearing in the early 13th century which dared to translate the Bible into the vernacular and, through unguided study, fell into such deadly errors as rejection of the Purgatory, of indulgences, of worship of saints and use of images, were decimated by ceaseless efforts of the defendants of the faith to obliterate the perverters of God's word. But the heresy still managed to survive, simply because the Waldences lived in the difficult to access mountainous terrain of Piedmont.

Sometimes it was the sheer number and fierce, organized armed resistance of the enemies of God, that would doom corrective measures to failure. Such was the case of the followers of one of the most notorious enemies of faith of the late fourteenth century, the Czech preacher John Hus. During his own theological studies, as well as while examining – carefully and critically – the works of his English contemporary, theologian John Wyclif, Hus decided that the ritual of the Eucharist ought to have been performed not only with bread, as was the common Church practice, but also with wine. For such thorough heresy and threat to the faith, Hus was excommunicated and his city, Prague, was put under the interdict. The threat to Prague was so imminent that Hus had to leave the city to spare it. And yet, the heretic felt that his views were legitimate and deserved serious consideration. In 1414 Hus, protected by the Emperor's safe-conduct, boldly arrived at the Church council of Constance to participate in deliberations of the clergy. But the faithful (whose main purpose in that meeting was to find a way out of the embarrassing schism of the Church caused by the existence of two popes, one in Rome, another in Avignion) could not tolerate the presence of an arrant perverter of God's will in their midst. Hus was arrested, tried for heresy, and burned at the stake. And while he was being burned, Hus was lucky enough to witness first-hand God's peculiar gift to the faithful: ineffable grace. It is told that an old woman bent with age came slowly along, dragging with effort a bunch of twigs and branches, and stopping by the fire, she added her load of fuel to the wood already burning the flesh of the enemy of God. Then Hus' eyes must have finally opened to the light of true faith. "Sancta simplicita!" – "Holy simplicity!" he exclaimed, struck by the holy beauty and purity of spirit of this woman, who – it must be admitted – was truly and exceptionally faithful, and was surely one of the greatest paragons of zealous belief, both before her time, and since. Heavy must have been the heart within Hus when he finally realized what holiness he was attempting to pervert with his Devil-inspired teaching! But it was too late to repent; the fire burned hot, and soon all was over.

(Hus was burned as a follower of Wyclif, and the trial that condemned Hus to death also ordered that Wyclif's remains be exhumed and burned. Wyclif was far more radical than Hus, and much to the regret of the defenders of the faith, they never managed to get a hold of him while he was alive. There was no Holy Inquisition in England, and all the appeals of the Pope were to no avail: Wyclif was protected by two of the most powerful barons of England – Edward, Prince of Wales, nicknamed the "Black Prince," and his brother John of Gaunt, Duke of Lancaster. Even much of the English clergy were on Wyclif's side, and on one occasion the faculty of Oxford, having examined his propositions, announced that, though some of them "sounded ill," they were "all the same true." The faithful had to be satisfied when Wyclif's remains were exhumed and burned in 1428 and his ashes thrown into the Swift river.)

But the trouble caused by Hus did not end with his death.

Hus was extremely popular in Bohemia, and when he was burned alive at the stake, his followers were outraged. The nobles pledged to defend Hus' reforms; the lower classes joined in. The Crusade, of course, was required to eradicate the heresy, and in 1417 Pope Martin V proclaimed a crusade against the Hussites. The heretics, who in the meantime found grounds for internal dispute, united and defeated the enormous army of crusaders. The second crusade of 1431 was a complete failure, too. The crusaders' army that comprised 90,000 infantry and 40,000 cavalry became dismayed, panicked, and ignominiously fled when it heard the approaching army of Hussites singing their battle hymn "All Ye Warriors of God." But the faith showed its power. The Hussites, though invulnerable to external pressure, became divided against themselves as they refined their views of God's will. The two opposing groups faced each other in battle in 1434. One of the armies was all but annihilated. Hussite movement survived for a few more decades till, in the early seventeenth century, it became marginal and was easily suppressed.

GERMAN CONFLAGRATION

The matter of Hus and his followers had been settled, but the Devil was strong and had many servants. A century after Hus died in the flames, big trouble started to the North of the Alps, in Germany. An obscure monk by the name of Martin Luther published some libelous and heretical propositions, scandalous to the faith. He was ranting that salvation could come only through personal faith, and so the Church with its rituals and ministrations was useless! He should have been arrested on the spot and burned at the stake before his Devilish proposition confused the believers. But alas, the secular authorities in his locality got so deluded by the heretic that, instead of doing their duty, they actually defended him and hid him from the hand of justice. Luther became so encouraged and felt so secure that, after being excommunicated by the Pope as an arrant heretic and enemy of faith, he burned the very bull which pronounced him a heretic, defying the Pope, God's deputy on Earth! The devil was strong indeed. Luther's heresy spread like wild fire.

Switzerland caught the contagion under the leadership of Calvin, and Sweden and England followed suit. Some regions of France were badly infected, too. The Night of St. Bartholomew of 1572, a successful surprise attack by French Catholics on the enemies of faith – French protestants called Huguenots – in which thousands of those perverted by the Devil had perished, brought some relief to the followers of the faith, and their morale soared high. But alas! It did not eradicate the heresy itself.

The history of what followed is well known and we will not recite it here. Foxe's "Book of Martyrs" gives a good idea of what was happening all over Europe: torture, hangings, beheadings, and burnings at the stake. "Wars of religion," – wars between the old and the new schools of faith to advance God's will – were ravaging Europe for decades. The continent had become a kind of hell. During the Thirty-year war alone, the population of Central Europe decreased almost by half. Meanwhile, the followers of the new, reformed Christianity soon discovered, just as their ancestors did a thousand years before them, how difficult it was for their fellow man to keep to the path of the faith. Unable to agree, the followers of reformed creed began to argue and divide among themselves. Reformed church quickly turned into Reformed Churches; Baptists, Calvinists, Unitarians, Mennonites, Arminians, and dozens of other smaller groups were soon united by not much more than their uncompromising and all-consuming hatred of the old

Church of Rome.

Some opinions, however, were so perverted that both the Holy Inquisition and the reformed believers were zealous in suppressing them. Michael Servetus, best known today for his discovery of a lesser or pulmonary circulation of blood, objected to the concept of Trinity. Both the Catholics and the Protestants were terrified by such a flagrant error. With the Inquisition in Catholic France on his heels, Servetus escaped to Calvinist Geneva, only to be apprehended, arrested, and burned at the stake by the reformed faithful, the mortal enemies of the Inquisition. Passions caused by interpretations of faith, and zeal for the advancement of God's will subsided only by the second quarter of the eighteenth century, when the war-weary Europeans finally agreed that matters of faith were better left to individuals themselves. This was a groundbreaking compromise, leading to the separation of church and state. Europe agreed to disagree in the matters of faith. The final afterglow of passions left by the fight for the faith continues to be felt in just a few places, like Northern Ireland.

MOSLEMS

STRONG BEGINNINGS

Moving onto the history of Islam, we discover that it, too, is in no way a stranger to religious infighting. In theory, Islam is less concerned with enforcing correct theological thinking on its adherents, striving rather to attain their proper behavior. Yet, though putting its emphasis on the way of life of the Moslems, Islam still has not managed to avoid violent conflicts – perhaps not so much through the disputes over finer points of theology, as over the general approach to it. Whatever the case, eagerness to advance God's will made Moslems go through quite a number of perturbations, all Islam's own.

Mohammed, the founder of Islam, lived through much derision and danger while trying to convince his neighbors of his prophetic mission, but ultimately he managed to gather a large group of loyal followers. His message spread, and by the end of his life he was by far the most powerful man in Arabia. His authority was immense. He was the living Word of Truth to the believers, and exercised unlimited spiritual and secular power over the faithful. They relied heavily on his guidance, which soon became indispensable. He was their ultimate example of proper behavior in this life, and their guide to the world to come. He was their link with God. They could always count on him to provide a just resolution of a dispute and a right answer to a difficult question. He guided them in times of war and peace. There existed among his followers a feeling of deep attachment to Mohammed. It was unthinkable to be without him, to be bereft of his insight and guidance.

SHIA AND SUNNI

And suddenly, the unthinkable happened. In 632 Mohammed died, leaving the faithful bereft and without a direct link with God. They were disconsolate, but found a way out of the crisis. They appointed a successor, or caliph, to Mohammed, to rule over them in his stead. Though the successor did not claim to have the gift of prophecy, he could still maintain and promote the values of Islam and advance its cause through the message left in the Koran, and by following Mohammed's way of life. Abu Bukr, the most respected person in the community and one of the first followers of Mohammed, was chosen to be the first caliph. But not everyone agreed with that choice. Some were sure that Mohammed had intended to pass his authority to his nephew and son-in-law, Ali. If that was the case – and to many, that was the case indeed – to obey anybody else but Ali would be to disobey the Prophet. It would be to go against God's will. The party, or *shiat*, supporting the rights of Ali gradually emerged. The faithful organized and rose up to fulfill God's will. What followed was essentially a series of uprisings and civil wars. The third caliph was killed, and Ali installed in his place, only to be murdered in his own turn. Ali's older son abdicated. His second son, however, bided his time and revolted, but was killed along with most of his relatives. For a while, events continued in a similar vein, and not many descendants of Mohammed managed to survive the fight for the faith. As a result, the party of Ali, having dwelt upon alleged injustice done to him and his sons for so long, began to attribute a globally fundamental importance to that episode in the political history of Islam. They began to see abrogation of the rights of the line of Ali as the capital crime against the faith. To them, the suppression of Ali's rights brought irreparable damage to Islam, since after Ali's death Moslems were guided by unauthorized leaders, leaders who had not been divinely endorsed. The faithful had been subjected to improper and, possibly, false guidance. The purity of faith had been completely compromised, for who knew to what wrong – or even godless – paths such divinely unauthorized guides had taken the faithful? To the Shiites, as the "party of Ali" came to be known, the martyred line of Ali became much more than mere unjustly slighted men. These martyrs started to loom as idealized, semi-divine figures, endowed with supernatural powers, who should yet come back and avenge themselves against their enemies. Shiites developed their own theology, heavily spiced with eschatological and messianic expectations. Defense of incorruptible purity of faith resulted in appearance of a stand-alone and highly militant branch of Islam.

SELFLESS ZEAL

All this happened in times long gone, but the spirit of valiant defense of God's will is very much alive and well among the present-day Moslems. Forgetting that the Arabs came to possess lands outside of the center of the Arabian peninsula through conquest (or, to use present-day Arab terminology, through "aggression and occupation") Palestinian Arabs decry Israel as encroachment upon "Arab land" and in attempts to destroy it, suicide bomb the Israelis. Their faith prompts and props their actions, promising the "martyrs" many sensual pleasures in paradise, envisioned as a chic bordello staffed with multiple "pure virgins" per customer. Motivated by Mohammed's injunction to "expel polytheists from the Arabian peninsula," Mr. Osama bin Laden interprets the presence of American troops in Saudi Arabia as a slap in the face of Islam and is doing his violent best to throw them out. His group has attacked Americans and other Westerners, as well as the Israelis, worldwide, bombing US army barracks at Khobar towers in Saudi Arabia, American embassies in Kenya and Tanzania, the USS Cole, and repeatedly, the World Trade Center in New York. In the first attempt, bin Laden's followers managed to kill five people and an unborn baby. The second attack, launched by suicide hijackers aiming also at the Pentagon and perhaps at the White House, destroyed the twin towers and killed three thousand people. As of the moment of this writing, Mr. Bin Laden, if still alive, is desperately seeking to obtain weapons of mass destruction to proceed in his battle for the faith on an even grander scale, towards the Final Solution of the American question.

PERFECT CITIZENS

PROLETARIAN HEAVEN

The faithful were ever zealous in unswerving defense of high Truth, but Truth has many forms. In the middle of the nineteenth century, a German economist by the name of Karl Marx discovered that human history was governed by laws as strict and inflexible as those which rule over the inanimate Nature. History, which on the surface seemed to result from collective actions of individuals, each guided by his or her personal ambitions and aspirations, in fact resulted from the action of the Law of Efficiency of Industrial Productivity. The political structure of any particular society, and the mentality of its members, were directly dependent upon the level of its economic development and sophistication of the means of production at its disposal. Human will, thought, and action were only superficially free. Actually, they were predetermined by the economic factors; an individual was something totally insignificant in itself. A certain level of development of productive machinery produced, for example, human relationships typical of feudal society, with its subservience of common folk to aristocracy and clergy; the more efficient machinery would cause the capitalist society to emerge, typified by a more democratic relationship between individuals. Mental and spiritual development of individuals comprising the society merely trailed behind such technological improvements. To think that human progress was driven by the thought and the spirit of individuals who envisioned and fought to bring about specific improvement of the political climate of their society was merely indicative of naïve, immature, shallow, "idealistic" thinking. Truly deep investigation clearly showed that all manner of spiritual activity such as literature, visual arts, science,

and political thinking trailed behind the development of productive machinery, and once the machinery got so developed
that the social structure and political system of a society could
no longer sustain the rate of technological growth, that social
order would become outdated and replaced by another, more
progressive one – usually through a violent revolution. Human
progress moves in revolutionary leaps and bounds, each leap
being caused by the development of productive technology
and resulting in a violent change of social structure and political system. Since human history was governed not by human
thoughts and passions, but by production of goods, history
should be thought of not in terms of specific individuals – that
would be naively and stupidly "idealistic," – but in terms of
"masses," that is, in the terms of "working class" engaged in
all-out "class struggle" against the "ruling class." That was the
methodology of Marx's "historical materialism." According to
it, capitalism was not the definitive and most progressive "socio-economic formation." In fact, it was in itself based upon
injustice and could not ensure the development of productive
machinery. Marx had discovered that capitalist entrepreneurs
indirectly appropriate a part of their employee's wages, taking
advantage of the ownership of industrial facilities. This was
the ultimate source of their huge wealth. The few were becoming very rich at the cost of the many. Such a situation was
not merely unjust; far more important was the fact that such
socio-economic order was not conducive to the production
of goods and the progress of History, since the workers did
not have a vital interest in the development of technology. But
if the workers would only unite, they could revolt and over-
throw the existing system of capitalist exploitation to establish
a just society in which production facilities would belong to the
workers themselves. Everyone would then get what he or she
actually earned. The productivity of a liberated worker would

then rise so high, and his love of free productive labor would become so great, that a great overabundance would result; every service and commodity would become free, money would be abolished with everybody living happily, taking what they need, producing what they can, contributing with the fruit of their creative labor to everyone's prosperity. History will hit a new stride. The new and ultimately just "socio-economic formation" of Communism will inevitably win the field.

That, of course, was the Truth: greedy capitalists were in the way of the progress of History and of Mankind's ultimate happiness. The struggle of the organized labor to improve conditions of the working class without removing the root of the evil that is private property, without appropriating the production facilities, was merely a feeble half-measure, only perpetuating the injustice. In fact, it was a betrayal of the fundamental interests of the working class and, much worse, it was hampering the advance of the next stage of History, it was stalling Progress. Accordingly, at the turn of the twentieth century, a group of Russians struck by the Truth of Marxist doctrine, became inflamed with the desire to see History moving and turned their outrage by the injustice done to the working class by capitalists and organized labor into a revolution that went all the way towards the Truth, Justice, and progress of History. In 1917 they overthrew the liberal provisional government that succeeded Czarist regime, and began to build a just and happy society of liberated workers.

First of all, they needed to get rid of the exploiters, of the rich who stood in the way of progress, as well as of the labor movement compromisers. This was easily accomplished. Those who had the means to flee, escaped abroad, and the rest had been dispossessed of their riches or killed. The communists took charge of the production and distribution of goods. But alas! Prosperity did not come. The Golden Age did not arrive.

Something went wrong. Apparently, the enemy had not been entirely killed off and continued to resist History's advance. This was a logical and lucky thought – for, as it turned out, the enemy penetrated every segment of society indeed: they were found among the army generals and among the highest-ranking ministers of state, as well as among the illiterate peasants and factory workers. Purges followed, and many of those who were known to have supported and organized the revolution proved to be "enemies of the people." They were apprehended and either "liquidated" or sent to labor camps by the millions. (Some historians count the enemy's numbers in the tens of millions.)

The accursed enemy even penetrated the ranks of those who were entrusted with guarding the greatest treasure there was in the world at the time – the health of the leader of workers of the world, comrade Stalin, the Teacher and the Leader, the living bearer of the Truth. (Luckily, those diabolically vicious monsters masking as doctors were extremely inefficient and, having had full access to the Leader for more than thirty years, were so tardy that they allowed him to die of natural causes in his good old age.) With so many enemies around, no wonder Communism never materialized. Today, after the collapse of the Soviet Union, the only legacy that communist worship of industrial production left to the new Russia is appalling poverty, corruption, and unprecedented environmental pollution.

THE HIGHEST RACE

Something quite similar happened in Germany. A person of high mind and noble spirit by the name of Adolf Hitler made a notable and noble discovery. He had discovered a new social Truth: the law of Race. His mind was too high to consider such a puny and insignificant thing as an individual, crawling somewhere worm-like in pursuit of his little personal happiness. Looking above the crowd, he realized that the world was populated by races of men, and that some of the races were great in the purity of their spirit, nobility of their thoughts, and healthiness of their physique, while others were groveling, earth-bound, capable only of base drives toward lucre and food, totally devoid of spirituality and nobility of purpose. Each race had its spirit and destiny, and each race had, hidden in its masses, a few choice individuals who perfectly exemplified it, who were filled with its spirit and with that spirit only, and who realized the destiny of their race and could lead the masses toward it. In fact, such an individual, and only he, the Leader, had the right to rule the Nation. Moreover, because the Leader was a perfect embodiment of his race, he knew better than anyone else what was good for it, and needed neither advice nor correction. It made perfect sense that his power was to be both absolute and undivided. The democratic process, based on such nonsense as justice and the rights and liberties of individuals – who were nothing in themselves, the race being all in all – was an idiotic invention of simpering weaklings, who could neither imagine nor raise themselves up to achieving the true grand destiny of the Race. The Leader had an innate ability and a natural right to rule. The Leader was the true personification of the race, a single, most pure bearer of its spirit; the race was one with the Leader in its thought and actions.

Once the political power legitimately belonging to the Leader was achieved, the first thing to do was to purify the Nation. In the course of history some migrations occurred, and members of foreign races were living among the native population, polluting it. Therefore, the foreigners – and especially the Jews (who, as the most careful and scientific investigations by the Nazi experts demonstrated, belonged to the lowest race imaginable) were to be eliminated from the midst of the Nation so that it could indeed start to breathe in the air of its own spirituality. With the contamination of the lower races removed, a new task awaited. To whichever race a person belongs, he eats, drinks, and occupies room on the face of the earth. The lowest eat as much as the highest. The lowest need as much room to live in as the highest. The cost of existence of the lowest is as high as that of the highest, but the benefit of the lowest to Mankind is negligible. Their culture is backward, if not degenerate. The lowest are just useless weeds, spread over vast territories that could be used by the Highest, with an incomparably greater benefit to Mankind. The surface of the planet being limited, it only made sense from the standpoint of Mankind's development that the finest race that represents Mankind at its best – the Aryans – should be given full advantage for growth and be allowed to move into the places most advantageous for habitation, while the lower races, for the benefit of Mankind, move out into the poorer spots and vacate room for the Better race.

In 1933 Mr. Hitler indeed managed to come to power, and he was as good as his word. Millions were exterminated by the Nazi zealots inspired by the light of the Truth. Those of the lowest race died in specially contrived gas chambers; many perished because they happened to occupy land needed by the Higher race. Many more were enslaved to work for the More Human.

The Higher race justly invaded the territories on which the lower races resided. Of course, the lower races, true to their base breeding, were selfish and did not care to sacrifice themselves to the Progress of Mankind. They were way too debased to even begin to comprehend the nobility of the great Truth discovered by the Leader of the Highest Race. They inconsiderately refused to obey the legitimate claims of the Higher race. They were so low and selfish that they would not vacate their territory, even though, in Truth, they were not entitled to it. But the Truth inspired the Higher race to great and noble deeds. Victorious armies of the Nazis were soon masters of most of Central and Western Europe, where they proceeded to exterminate the Lowest by the millions. Then they moved East, into Russia. But, as it turned out, even the Highest race had a limit to its potential. Resistance of the low-bred Russians to the Nazi armies that advanced under the ensigns of Truth, Progress, and Light of Civilization, was most dogged and stubborn. Americans and the British, staunch advocates of debased ideas of human rights and democracy, joined the fight against the Highest race from the West. By the year 1943 the tide had turned; in 1944 the beastly herds of lower races were defiling the sacred soil of the Fatherland of Aryans with their unholy feet. In a year, everything was over. The leadership of the Higher race had a chance to cool off from their frenzied and hysterical rhetoric and listen from their benches at the Nuremberg Trial to what the rest of mankind had to say of their theories and of the practices inspired by them.

Chapter 2

Who is at Fault?

WESTERNER'S DILEMMA

Oceans of human blood have been spilled in fulfilling God's will and advancing high Truth. The fact is well supported by history and cannot be disputed. In the past, bloody exploits in enforcing God's will were a source of pride to the religious – why else would Abraham's zeal in attempting to sacrifice his son, or the butchery that followed the making of the golden calf, or king Saul's genocide of Amalekites become such a prominent part of God's word? In some parts of the world the faithful still take pride in such acts, as evidenced by quite a bit of rejoicing and dancing on the 11th of September, 2001 throughout the Middle East. The present-day West, however, has different sensitivities and recoils at the sight of blood in horror and dismay. Today's Westerner finds violence hardly justifiable at all, and completely inappropriate as a means of expressing religious fervor. Being a strictly peaceful creature, he just cannot bear the thought that spilling blood has anything to do with belief in God. He cannot bring himself to think that the religion that he respects as a major manifestation of mankind's spirituality and high-mindedness can cause violence that is the very incarnation of bestiality. Yet, he cannot deny that sometimes the love of God is being expressed through bloodshed. In order to get around the unpleasant implications of religious violence, he needs to have religion disentangled from violence – how else can he hold dear what has been soiled by blood and murder?

Luckily, there is a simple way for him to do as he desires. No religion supports violence, he assures us. If religion appears to be encouraging bloodshed, he tells us, we witness perversion of religion, not the genuine article itself. In his view, violent fellows are not real believers. Real believers do not kill; real believers do not cause suffering. Tragedies would not have happened had the so-called believers been indeed true to the spirit of their religion, rather than just paying lip service to it, we are told.

EVIL-DOERS AND CYNICS

This argument was fully used, for example, to explain the attack of September 11th, when America and the rest of the western world were forced to come to grips with the fact that religion-inspired violence is alive and well – and is threatening each and every one of us. In editorial after editorial, in speech after speech, our newspapers and our political leaders pounded us with this explanation. Osama bin Laden and his subordinates put a good thing to bad use by misinterpreting and corrupting it. Islam, this good and peaceful religion, had been hijacked by evil, inhumane, and soulless rascals. They brainwashed innocent, impressionable youths with a corrupt interpretation of religion, instilled in them uncompromising hatred of the West and, having tempted them with pleasures of paradise, they made them ready and willing to give up their lives in order to destroy America. Of course, the terrorists were not real believers, they were not real Moslems. They just perverted the faith and cynically used it to attain their political ends.

Such dismissive argument is well known, and is used whenever there is a need to disentangle the knot binding a specific ideology to the violence it fosters. Years ago, I was surprised to discover in New York a bookstore which specialized in books by Lenin, Mao, and the like. Naively, I thought that the well-known facts of political oppression and murder practiced by regimes based on Marxism would disenchant anyone with it. I asked a young gentleman running the store if he had ever heard of Gulag or of Cultural Revolution. Surprise! Surprise! He actually had. So how he could be selling such stuff – and who buys it? "Oh, that's simple," he told me. "The Soviets were not true revolutionaries. If true revolutionaries were running the world, nothing of the kind would have happened." In another conversation, a missionary told me that faith in Jesus makes people gentle, peaceful, and loving. "Well, how about the Inquisition?" I asked him. "Oh, they weren't true Christians," he replied.

This is a good, solid, convenient explanation. One can be sure that, at times, this explanation is even adequate. At times – but not always. As we have seen, Abraham, this paragon of faith, almost killed his own son to please God. St. Augustin flogged Nubian Christians who advocated adult baptism into agreeing with the True doctrine – and had their property confiscated if they persisted in error. Martin Luther, mindful of the scriptural commandment to "not suffer a witch to live," burned at the stake thousands of ladies, both young and old. John Calvin, not to be left behind, also burned not a few heretics. Yet, how many of us would dare call Abraham, St. Augustin, Martin Luther, and John Calvin "soulless, evil monsters," cynically misusing religion or corrupting it for their private ends?

THE PURE IN HEART
AND THE POOR IN SPIRIT

In fact, it can be argued that these individuals, and the crowds they led, were whom Jesus lauded as the "pure in heart" and the "poor in spirit" in his celebrated Sermon on the Mount. He assured us that the former are "blessed for they shall see God," while the latter are "blessed for theirs is the kingdom of heaven." It is instructive to pause for a second and reflect on the definition of the "pure in heart" and "poor in spirit." Traditionally, heart symbolizes the seat of one's feelings, emotions, and, most importantly, of one's loyalties, attachments, and love. By talking of those "pure in heart," I think Jesus must have meant the individuals whose loyalty to God is uncontaminated by any earthly interest. Their faith is pure and sincere. They are willing to study God's word and follow God's directions wherever He takes them – just as Abraham, the greatest paragon of purity in heart, did. Their purity in heart allows them to clearly see God's will in His word, their spiritual sight easily penetrating through the mist of human passions like love, pity, prudence, or common sense, and giving them the ability to guide others in the direction of godliness. Pure in heart individuals are those who lead the faithful in their progress to salvation. St. Augustin, Luther, Calvin, and the like certainly fall under this category. Lenin and Hitler, in their own way, show every symptom of purity in heart, too.

The dominant trait of the poor in spirit, on the other hand, seems to be the innate intellectual simplicity, perhaps even naïveté, which makes them poor leaders yet excellent followers. Though incapable of abstract thinking and analysis, their emotional make-up and natural sincerity make them eager to embrace the faith, even if they do not understand its niceties and finer points. They are simple and unlearned but have good hearts and are eager to help bring closer the Kingdom of God in whichever way they can.

The history we've just surveyed appears to have been enacted by these two groups, by the pure in heart and the poor in spirit. They seem to constitute the core of organizers of every movement of the faithful. The pure in heart supply the ideology, exercise the leadership, outline the goals and come up with strategies to achieve these goals. The poor in spirit, having imbibed such basics of ideology which their essential intellectual simplicity allows them to digest, enthusiastically undertake fulfillment of the task at hand – and bring unbearable suffering and misery into the world.

So, the argument of violence-abhorring Westerners, that bloodshed is a perversion rather than fulfillment of religion, appears to be far from convincing. One could call it a lame and simplistic explanation produced by wishful thinking, and not be too harsh.

MASKS AND FACES

Well, much can be said for either side of this debate, especially if we allow ourselves to be dragged into the murky area of human psychology that motivates our actions. Luckily, however, there is no need to get into an argument. The reason is simple: motivations are totally irrelevant. Let us not forget that we live in a world where actions count, not the intentions. It makes but little difference to the victims and their families and friends that the fire was set, the trigger was pulled, or the bomb was exploded by a cynical hypocrite masking as a believer, rather than by a genuinely believing person. Though cynicism and hypocrisy undoubtedly played some role, the actors on the scene of history moved strictly within the frameworks of their respective faiths. In fact, this is precisely what made them successful. Religion lent itself to their purposes extremely well. What difference does the "true" intention make if the actions of a cynic, a hypocrite, and a believer are identical? Abbot Arnald-Amalric's famous "Kill them all; God will look after His own" may sound ominously cynical to us, but it could have been said by the sincerest believer, from whose standpoint this approach makes perfect sense. Let Abraham, St. Augustine, Luther, Calvin, Stalin, Hitler be cynics rather than believers – what changes? The fires of the Inquisition, the gas chambers of the Nazi Third Reich, and the Gulags and mass executions by the Communists all made perfect sense within the framework of theoretical thought that inspired and instituted them in the first place. The "real" purposes are simply irrelevant to the resulting action, since each specific action can be fully justified within the framework of religion by whose overt blessing it had been performed, no matter what were the private motivations of actual participants.

The same goes for hypocrites. Of course, a good many hypocritical opportunists have undoubtedly found it advantageous to mix into the crowd of the genuine poor in spirit in order to gain some temporal benefits and feather their nests; yet, what does it change? In fact, not many had a choice. Keeping to one's own opinion in societies not particularly appreciative of personal liberties was a dangerous option; not to fall victim to the poor in spirit, it was better to become one of them. Under such circumstances, hypocrisy simply became a chief means of survival for those indifferent to a given Truth or for the individuals with views of their own. As we have seen, Galileo hypocritically rescinded his views, because he knew what price was put on personal integrity by the pure in heart. Galileo's English contemporary, one Bartholomew Legate, a "person comely, complexion black, of a bold spirit, confident carriage, fluent tongue, exceedingly skilled in Scriptures," would not compromise. Arrested in 1612 because he denied divinity of Jesus, he was for two years visited in prison by clerics who tried to help him out of his ways of error. King James of England, famous today for authorizing an English translation of the Bible that became a classic, would himself come to Bartholomew's cell and personally plead with him. Hypocrisy would have easily led him out of prison, but, be it prudent or not, this was not the way of Bartholomew Legate. He knew the price, and was willing to pay it. On March 13 of 1614, he was burned at the stake. On the other hand, Isaac Newton, one of the greatest scientists the world had ever known, also held Unitarian views but was most careful to keep them to himself.

Situations where it was safe to display sincerity were few and far between – and always striking as examples of personal bravery and disregard of danger. One such example will suffice. Once, during Orthodox Easter, Czar Nicolas I of Russia (who was so pure in heart that he suppressed Russian translation of the Bible, fearing that excessive study might mar the innocent faith of his subjects, and was so eager to save the Jews that he ordered them drafted into the army, almost in infancy, to prevent the perverse influence of their family's religion) while passing through his palace, greeted a sentinel at the door with the traditional Orthodox Easter greeting, "Christ is risen." To his utter amazement, the sentinel shouted back, in the stilted way of the Russian military, "not-at-all-your-Imperial-majesty!" When he recovered his breath, the Czar demanded an explanation. The sentinel replied that he was Jewish and could not conscientiously admit that Christ had risen. And guess what? Nicolas was so pleased that he had the chance to experience a new, for him, sensation of being contradicted, that he gave the soldier a valuable present. In that particular case everything went well, and yet that soldier's Jewishness gave his rejection of Christ an aura of legitimacy. If he were a Russian peasant, however, and told Nicolas that he arrived at that conclusion through a personal study of the Bible, the story could have had quite a different ending – and far from a happy one, too. He would have had a fair chance of sharing the fate of Bartholomew Legate – or at least would have been sent to Siberia. He would have been far better off keeping his mouth shut, even if that meant being a hypocrite. Hypocrisy would help him stay out of trouble, to survive.

It was the hypocrite's ability to imitate the sincerest and most genuine pure in heart and poor in spirit perfectly, to look exactly like them, to talk exactly like them, to act exactly like them, that allowed so many to survive and thrive at times when ardor for Truth was holding sway. Hypocrisy is a result of this ardor, and hypocrites are its victims. They are not in any way, shape, or form a cause of atrocities committed to advance the Truth, though they certainly had a hand in them.

However it may be, it would have been hard, if at all possible, to make Abraham, King Saul, St. Augustine, Luther, Calvin, Stalin, Hitler, or Osama bin Laden confess to cynicism or hypocrisy. If pressed to answer for the blood they shed, they would probably insist that they followed the will of God, or that they aimed at the Highest Truth. To make them acknowledge that they misunderstood God's word, that they mistook the Truth, that they perverted religion, that they were driven by "evil" would be, one suspects, the ultimate exercise in futility.

EVIL OR ERROR?

So, rather than wasting time in dissecting psychology of people like Abraham, Saul, St. Augustine, Luther, Calvin, Stalin, Hitler, or Osama bin Laden and proving them "evil," we are better off just accepting them at their word. They acted with assurance of following God's will, or worked to advance some other high Truth. The problem is, of course, that their good intentions turned to proverbial flagstones that pave the road to Hell; yet, explanations for this paradox advanced so far are hardly satisfactory. To call those who cause suffering "evil ones" is the easiest thing in the world to do, but such "explanation" simply dismisses the problem rather than help us understand what is going on. "Evil" describes something that is out of our control and is beyond our understanding. By calling something "evil" we acknowledge that more is going on than human reasoning can explain, and, for all practical purposes, wash our hands of the problem. We give up fighting the adversary with corrective ideas and turn instead to physically wiping the enemy out with missiles and bombs.

Though military response is often an unfortunate necessity, we should not so quickly give up on understanding what is going on in the enemy's mind.

Here is why: one does not need to be "evil" in order to cause terrible suffering to innocent people. Results of an honest mistake in assumptions that underpin a perfectly good and worthy endeavor can be exactly identical to disasters caused by genuine evildoers. It is impossible to tell from results alone whether they were caused by evil, or by error.

In 1986 the space shuttle Challenger exploded during the launch, and all astronauts were killed. Was NASA "evil"? Such was not the conclusion of the committee that investigated the disaster. It turned out that the launch occurred during freezing temperatures, and the rubber became brittle and caused fuel to leak, resulting in an inferno. Not "evil" at work, but human error. That same year, Soviet nuclear scientists staged a bit of a scientific experiment using one of the reactors at the Chernobyl power plant. It resulted in the worst ecological disaster in human history. And again, it turned out that Soviet nuclear scientists were not "evil;" they did not conspire to produce such a horrific event. They simply made a wrong assumption.

Perhaps something similar is causing religious violence, too. If such is the case, Osama bin Laden and his ilk are sincere, well-meaning people who cause misery because their underpinning assumptions are wrong.

This is something we can deal with. While it is beyond our powers to understand evil, we should be up to the task of uncovering a mere human error.

Actions of the pure in heart and poor in spirit can be described by a very simple formula: Zeal in pursuit of Truth brings Disaster. Two parts of this equation are not variables. Sincerity of zeal is irrelevant. The disaster it brings is obvious – it has manifested itself through terrible bloodshed on way too many occasions. The only variable left unexamined is the Truth.

Let us presently turn to this stumbling block of the pure in heart.

CHAPTER 3

PURSUIT OF TRUTH

How do We Know?

Defining truth, as well as ascertaining it, is the most interesting and puzzling problem that confronts mankind. That we should be confronted with such a problem is a natural result of the fact that each of us is not the sole object existing in the Universe. There are many things existing outside of an individual: there are other people, there are animals, there are inanimate objects, there are natural forces and natural phenomena, and we need to understand how these outside things impact us. This is a vital need rather than a matter of pure curiosity, since our very existence depends on reliable evaluation of objects that surround us. Is it too cold to venture outdoors? Is my jacket warm enough to go out? Does the approaching dog want to bite me? Do I have enough money for the trip I plan? Where does this train go? If I do not feel well, what is the matter with me? Which pill should I take? All these, and a myriad of other, similar questions confront us every split second of our lives, and getting adequate answers is vital to our very existence.

Since these objects exist outside of ourselves, we cannot simply look into our minds to discover their nature. Our minds will not be able to generate the required information. When we want to go into the street and need to know the outside temperature, thinking about the temperature is not going to help us. We can meditate for days and nights, for weeks, months, and years on end, and still have no clue as to what to wear. We can learn about something only from that something itself. We learn about it by reaching out to it, by sampling it with the help of our senses of sight, hearing, smell, touch, and taste and by passing the reactions of our senses to the mind. To learn the outside temperature, we should open a window and feel the air with our hand, or look at the outdoor thermometer, or listen to the weather forecast – and our senses of touch, sight, and hearing will give us the information we seek.

This in not to say that information received through our senses is always perfectly adequate. The object whose nature we are probing may posses some crucially important properties that our senses are unable to detect. We cannot feel dangerous radioactive radiation, for one, nor can we see bacteria and germs. Poison may taste as sweet as the most delicious and nutritious food. By getting sensorial impressions of objects, we absorb only the picture of the object, not the object itself. That picture, of course, allows us to generate some sort of judgment about it, but that judgment will always be of a merely "some sort" kind, reliable to a degree, perhaps adequate for our purposes, hopefully holding no unpleasant surprises in store. There can be no guarantee that our judgment does full justice to the object under investigation, that it leaves none of its properties and functions unlearned, or that the properties which it does describe, are described adequately. In other words, there is never a guarantee that our opinion about the object that is reached through the use of our senses is the Truth. Our mind comes up with a picture that appears acceptably adequate to us, but that is its limit. In all our investigations, we get only what is acceptable, not necessarily what is true.

Yet, having said that, we cannot gainsay that we have a great deal of very reliable information. After all, we do know enough to have airplanes, telephones, and computers. Perhaps the situation is not that gloomy; perhaps there is no need to give up our claims on the Truth.

To answer, it is important to understand how we arrived at our present state of knowledge. The discovery and harnessing of the laws of nature that allowed us to have the comforts and amenities of civilized life was a slow process. It took many thousands of individuals of most uncommon, and often exceptional, ability – mathematicians, physicists, chemists, and engineers – hundreds of years of research and experiment to discover these laws and find ways of putting them to use. It was a long and devious road, marked by many mistakes and disappointments, and crowned by many triumphs. Progress was very gradual. To use a simple example, the first scientist who attempted to determine the shape of the Earth decided that it must be flat. That agreed well with his experiment, which consisted of looking down at the ground and observing a perfectly flat surface. That, at the time, was the "last word" of science. Another scientist, living a few generations later, looked around and noticed the horizon line that cannot be explained away if one assumes that the Earth is flat, and realized that our planet was a globe. His conclusion advanced science tremendously; yet brilliant as he must have been, he also believed the Earth to be the center of the universe, with the Sun and planets and the firmament of little bright stars revolving around it. His research was followed by some very detailed observations of the motions of celestial bodies. The astronomical data made it crystal clear that Earth moved along with the rest of the planets around the Sun, not the other way around. Further observations demonstrated that the multitude of little bright stars in the night sky, thought originally to be tinsel put there by God, just to enliven the view of the sky from the Earth, and to give a bit of additional light to us at night, were in fact enormous galaxies, tens of thousands of light years in size consisting of millions, perhaps billions of suns, and located at enormous distances from the Earth. And so it was with many other phenomena. Year after year, scientists studied Nature. Isaac Newton discovered the law of gravitation; Michael Faraday researched the phenomena of electricity and magnetism; James Clerk Maxwell gave mathematical description of electromagnetic waves. Natural and artificial radioactivity had been discovered, paving the way for the creation of the atomic bomb and for modern investigation into the structure of an atom. Einstein advanced a new global theory of the Universe, which was more precise than Newton's; Eddington confirmed it by direct observation of the trajectory of the rays of starlight passing by the Sun during a complete solar eclipse. Inventors and industrialists used the knowledge gained in all branches of science to produce useful gadgetry, of which telephones, airplanes, and computers are some typical examples.

All this development did not happen in one day or one year. It takes time to refine our information about the outside world. It is a very slow process indeed: extraction of knowledge requires performing multiple experiments over and over again in order to ascertain different facets of the phenomenon and to inspect it from many different angles and points of view. It requires detailed, careful, and unhurried study. It requires analysis of experimental data. It requires advancing and verification of plausible theories. All these processes are time-consuming, and it is critical for the success of any particular investigation that the object or phenomenon that is being investigated be accessible for the whole duration of the research. Men were able to ascertain the shape of the Earth only because the Earth was around for thousands of years, ever since man began to think. We were able to accumulate all the facts we now know about Nature and its laws precisely because the natural phenomena were always within our reach, always allowing people with an inquisitive mind to examine them, always lending themselves to experiments. Thousands of researchers were being able to experiment, draw conclusions, integrate them into theories and check whether the yet-unknown phenomena which should have been observable if their theories were true, were observable indeed. They could test their theories and repeat their experiments for hundreds of years, thus digging deeper and deeper into the nature of things and refining our knowledge further and further.

But such convenient availability of phenomena for research is not always the case. Some phenomena are transient, and their limited availability for study makes it extremely difficult, if at all possible, to investigate them. How are we to draw definite conclusions about an object that looks like a flying saucer, crosses the nightly sky, and vanishes within a second? For all we know, it can be an alien spaceship, it can be a large meteor, it can be a result of some atmospheric perturbation, it can be a vision caused by our mental state, or it can be almost anything. Many possibilities are open; we can guess all we want and advance as many theories as we wish, but there is no clear answer – nor can there be. Since the duration of our access to that mysterious object was extremely brief, it is impossible to say anything definitive about it, and its true nature will forever remain a mystery. The insufficient time period during which a particular object is available for research, or the difficulty of accessing it at any given moment may spell the doom of any attempt to gain adequate information about it.

HISTORICAL TRUTH

It may not really matter to a physicist, who can always repeat his experiment. But to a historian, it makes all the difference in the world. Time flies. Events occur and are no more.

As time passes, events become permanently inaccessible for research. This is the intrinsic, inherent problem of research in history. Of course, the technological power of the second half of the twentieth century makes the work of future historians much easier and far more reliable. They will always be able to witness major events through piles of video recordings. They will not need to rely on scant hearsay when studying the stages of the impeachment trial of President Clinton, for example. They will be able to sit back, look at a TV screen, and re-live the whole drama, minute after minute and day after day, from the first appearance of the scandalous news to the final stage of the justice done. They will be always able to stop the VCR when they need to think; they will be always able to go back or move ahead, just as the need of their thesis drives them. That part of History will become a frozen-in-time and ever-accessible Fact.

The less conspicuous events pass unnoticed, however. The simplest practical consequence of that fact is the work of our criminal justice system. If we had perfect knowledge of history, we would have known with precision every circumstance and every perpetrator of any particular crime, and it would be easy to administer perfect justice. But that, unfortunately, is not the case. Because we do not have precise knowledge of the events as they happened, we can only do our best through a cumbersome and quite inefficient trial by jury. The jury will pronounce a suspect guilty only if it is presented with sufficient evidence. Thus, if a criminal did a really clean job and left no clues as to his identity, he will never be caught, or will not be convicted. If the evidence happens to point to a person who is innocent, that person may be convicted of a crime he has never committed. Much effort was spent in one of the most celebrated recent criminal cases, that of O. J. Simpson, but the adequacy of its outcome was doubted by many. This would not have been the case if we had sufficient access to the historical events: there would be no need for a trial by jury, and a judge's decision would always be fully adequate.

If the future historian, having finished his studies of the impeachment of President Clinton, would turn to the study of some less conspicuous event of our history which did not happen to attract the attention of the press at the time it occurred, his efforts will be baffled because no first-hand, completely reliable information would be available. That is the case of many events of the more distant past. As historians move into areas buried deeper in the mists of time, they find less and less reliable material that can help them to bring to life the events of Time Past. Though some documents may be found, they are often way too scanty, way too sketchy, way too subjective, way too unreliable, way too inadequate to build a coherent and reliable picture of the events. Only some vague, generalized, and uncertain statement can be made, with hope, but without certainty, that it is at all adequate.

Of course, were it possible to build Herbert Wells' Time Machine, a historian would have as reliable a source of information as a physicist does. He would be able to travel back in time and witness the events that interest him, for himself. Just as in physics, where every skeptic can repeat any experiment and become convinced that a certain physical phenomenon indeed exists, every skeptical historian would be able to take a trip into the past and check whether Plato was right about the foundered civilization of Atlantis, or watch the exact method of erection of the pyramid of Heops, or bring home, as a pleasant souvenir of the trip, a photograph of Helen the Beautiful pensively watching the movement of Greek armies from the tall and mighty ramparts of Troy. The lovers of literature would stop arguing about the authorship of Shakespeare plays: they would be able to actually see Shakespeare – or Lord

Bacon, for that matter – putting down on paper the immortal lines of Hamlet and King Lear, and would quickly learn the exact identity, and study the features of the enigmatic Dark Lady of the Sonnets. Art scholars would be able to get a perfect chronology of each artist's work and photograph the works of art lost in the course of history. Exercising justice would become a much easier task, too, since the Time Machine would have enabled the judge to eyewitness the crime and establish the identity of a criminal and guilt or innocence of a suspect beyond the slightest shadow of a doubt.

But this is just wishful thinking. Much to our regret, we do not have the Time Machine, and are not likely to ever build one. We cannot inquire into history the way we can inquire into Nature. We do not have fully reliable sources of historical information; our sources run the full gamut from almost reliable to completely unreliable, from videotapes and voice recordings to hearsay. We can never be sure that a certain event indeed occurred in reality and not in the glib imagination of the author of an ancient book that describes it. And if that event had indeed occurred, we still cannot be sure the ancient historian gave us an adequate picture of its causes, or that the event was as important as he would have us believe. And we can be sure that there have been many defining moments in the history of mankind, of which we know absolutely nothing. To summarize, much of the historical information is irrevocably lost and much is uncertain past redemption.

Having learned this much about the extent and reliability of our knowledge of history, let us return to the pure in heart and poor in spirit zealous in advancement and defense of the Truth. As we have seen, reliability of information about any particular phenomenon directly depends on its availability for research, and all information could be divided into the "verifiable," (when it pertains to natural sciences), and the "nonverifiable" (in cases of historical information). Our question becomes, to what class does the Truth defended by the pure in heart and poor in spirit belong? How did they arrive at it? Are their claims based on something that is accessible and available for study permanently and repeatedly, as in physics, or just for a single passing moment, as in history?

Social theories like Communism and Nazism are based on the study of society and, superficially, seem to possess objectivity typical of the natural sciences. But, unlike Nature, which stays essentially static – at least for some five thousand years it had been an object of human study – society itself changes constantly, and in a very real way. People who comprise it gradually pass away to be replaced by completely different individuals, their children, and their grandchildren. Each succeeding generation brings its own ideas and attitudes, making society of today very different from that of a hundred, not to speak of, a thousand years ago, both in its physical make-up and in mental attitudes. A social theory that may seem adequate today is out of touch tomorrow. Moreover, speculative Truths like Communism and Nazism take a supra-human, global perspective that renders them totally irrelevant as far as an individual is concerned. But each of us leads an individual existence, and we can be grouped only in some conventional and artificial, rather than real, sense, and all the talk of "races," "nations," and "classes" is ultimately meaningless, as is the advancement of their "progress."

On the other hand, religions of Judaism, Christianity, and Islam all claim to be based on historic events. Miracles are supposed to have proven the divine origin of revelation that formed Judaism and Christianity some four and two millennia ago respectively; ultimate revelation presumably given to Mohammed some fourteen hundred years ago props the zeal of fighters for the Truth of Islam.

As we have seen, delving in long-gone history is a murky business that produces highly unreliable results. Therefore, we cannot be too sure of the parting of the Red Sea, of walking on the water, or of the water turned to wine. The very nature of history tells us to be cautious and to take all such highly unusual events with a big grain of salt. The pure in heart and poor in spirit would have saved the world a good deal of bloodshed and suffering had they taken the time to reflect on the treacherousness of historical "Truth."

REVEALED TRUTH

But the central pillar of major religions, of course, is the Revelation. Those of the Jewish faith are sure that some four thousand years ago God revealed Himself to Moses and that later on, He spoke through the mouths of Isaiah, Jeremiah, and other Jewish prophets. Christians claim that they got a portion of their Truth through God's son Jesus, the rest through the divinely inspired St. Paul. Moslems tell us that Mohammed was the Seal of the Prophets, the last prophet of God to ever grace the Earth, who passed God's ultimate will to mankind.

How do we approach such claims? Dismissing them out of hand would be wrong, for Revelation may indeed have happened. Embracing them would be just as wrong, for, as with other highly unusual and unverifiable events, there can be no guarantee that it actually occurred. We are faced with a curious dilemma that can be described as a "problem of the third party."

The problem is easy to describe. Bob runs into Charlie and tells him what Annie just said. That's all there is to it. The second party tells the third party that he just spoke to the first party, and passes on to that third party the contents of his or her conversation with the first one. There is nothing unusual about it. Each of us has many times been in a position of either one of those three parties. Few words dropped in a casual conversation with an acquaintance were duly reported by him to another mutual friend, thus turning us into the first party. In a discussion among the friends, we would occasionally quote someone not present at the moment, becoming a second party of the dilemma. And now and then we have received plenty of report from our good friends on the opinions of some other persons of acquaintance, making us the third party. Usually, the information passed in this way is so trivial and unimportant that we forget it just as quickly as we receive it. At times, however, it is of considerable relevance to us, and we want to have it verified at its source. Nothing can be simpler. With plenty of means of communication available to us, from a face to face conversation to the telephone and e-mail, confirmation and verification – or, for that matter, denial – of what has been told by the second party is fairly easy. We all have been through this too many times to count; "did you really say that?" is not an infrequently asked question.

Now, all this works very smoothly indeed – until one of the links of this chain falls out. What if the first party is not available to the third? How can the third party make sure that the second party tells us the truth? It has no means of verification. How can the third party even be sure that the second party spoke to the first one at all, that it was not a mistake or the figment of imagination of the second party, not to speak of willful misrepresentation of facts? There can be no guarantees. Yet, this is a typical situation at the time of inception of a prophetic religion. When the first party is God, the second party is the prophet, and the third party is the general public, the third party cannot go directly to the First, and there is no way of verifying veracity of the second. Worse, there is no way to even know that the second party was ever in contact with the First – there is no guarantee that the prophet spoke to God indeed; he may have misidentified his interlocutor. What if not only is the First party unavailable to the third, but the second party had suddenly disappeared too? There is no longer a way for the third party to get authoritative clarification of the words of the second party uttered while it was around. Members of the third party must now be content with whatever interpretation of the petrified record left by the second party he or she can come up with. Sounds like chaos? Well, this is a typical situation of the mature state of prophetic religion, its period after the prophet dies – the time of heresies and schisms.

Islam, as a straightforward religion based on the teachings of a single prophet, provides an excellent illustration of the paradoxes resulting from the problem of the third party, and its grim consequences. Take the first state of Islam, for instance. When Mohammed stated that "Koran is God's word", and when anyone else (his close follower and first caliph Abu Bukr, for example) stated that "Koran is God's word," we have two identically-sounding yet completely different statements. Mohammed, as a self-proclaimed second party, may or may not have been receiving God's word and so, to a degree, was justified in making his statement; Abu Bukr or anyone else of the third party was in no position to know whether it was God whispering into Mohammed's ear, and had no right to make his statement. Mohammed could be called a spiritual person; Abu Bukr or anyone else, as we shall see, is nothing but an idolater. So, paradoxically, the problem of the third party turns exactly the same words coming from the different mouths into very different, if not opposite, messages.

Islam's second phase came when Mohammed died and became inaccessible, and Moslems faced the issue of succession. Did Mohammed appoint Ali to be his successor as some claimed, or did he not? The actors in the problem of the third party now change from God-Mohammed-population to Mohammed as the first party, those around him who heard Mohammed endorse (or not endorse) Ali as the second one, and the general population as the third. The result, as we saw, was a bloody split of Islam into the shiah and the sunni factions.

Where does all this lead us in our pursuit of revealed Truth?

For one, there is no such thing as "true spirit of religion," imagined by the peace-loving, violence-abhorring western believers; nor, it must be said to their horror, is the violence a perversion of religion. Everything is just a matter of interpretation. Each religion passes through two stages. In the first stage, its founder is alive. Everyone who wishes to partake of the putative word of God, to know of His presumed will, must come to the prophet. The prophet has all the say, the believer has none. The second stage arrives after the prophet dies. All of a sudden, a paradoxical role reversal takes place. The prophet goes silent, just as the public was before his passing; yet God's putative word, liberated by the death of the prophet, becomes public property and passes into everyone's domain. Anyone who cares can now seize on the record of God's word and become a mouthpiece of God's will by interpreting the text any way he or she wishes, reading into it anything he or she wants. Anyone now wields prophetic powers once restricted only for the use of the founder of the religion. Scripture becomes a smokescreen behind which one can, with total impunity, attribute to God just about anything he or she feels is "God's word." And corresponding action follows, too. It is in human nature to do what is right. And what God says is, by definition, right. What the scripture says is, by definition, what God says. Scripture is to be followed – the way one understands it. There is no other way, in fact, once the second party of the revelation passes on. Violence will follow from the ones who understand the revelation as demanding war on the infidels. Peace and acts of charity will come from the ones who see it as requesting peace and acts of charity. And no action will follow at all from those who see in it a demand for inactive contemplation.

Once the founding father of a religion dies, the religion that he has founded effectively ends, to become replaced by multiple religions of more or less uniform character. There is no longer a Judaism but as many Judaisms as there are Jews that care. Christianity is gone, to become replaced by as many Christianities as there are Christians. And there are as many Islams as there are Moslems in the world. Talking of any particular religion in general terms, without qualifying whose interpretation is being presented, is pure nonsense. U. S. President George W. Bush reads the Koran and tells us that Islam is a religion of peace. Osama bin Laden reads the Koran and yells "kill them all!" Most intriguingly, both men are right: Bush's Islam is peaceful; Osama's is violent. Whether the "true" Islam – Islam as Mohammed envisioned it – is peaceful or violent, no one can possibly know.

Of course, one could point out that in some traditions God, the First party of revelation, is not at all inaccessible to the public that constitutes the third party. One could claim that there still are individual revelations, that all one needs to do is to search for God with his whole heart and soul, to ask Him to reveal Himself. There are many who feel they've been born again after undergoing a transforming experience of communication with God. Basically, they are telling us that they became a second party. It must be pointed out that such experience is as unreliable as was the original revelation to the founding prophet, and is a legitimate subject of doubt by anyone else. But to be fair, let us give this argument a benefit of the doubt and examine the mechanics of attaining such revelation. The result is disappointing. The believer asks to confirm what is a foregone conclusion that Jesus is his savior, and does not stop praying until the desired revelation is received, literally cornering his or her own mind in the process. At least, this is the impression from examining the first-hand account given by the great evangelical writer, John Bunyan. Here is how one of the heroes of his classical book "The Pilgrim's Progress" relates to another one his actions, after learning through the study of the scripture and from a conversation with a friend, that unless Jesus saves him through grace, he is doomed to the fires of hell:

"– ...Then I asked him, what must I do...? And he told me, I must entreat upon my knees, with all my heart and soul, [God] the Father to reveal him [Jesus] to me.... I told him that I knew not what to say.... And he bid me say to this effect: 'God be merciful to me a sinner' and 'make me know and believe in Jesus Christ....'

– And did you do as you were bidden?

– Yes, over, and over, and over.

– And did the Father reveal the Son to you?

– Not at the first, nor second, nor third, nor fourth, nor fifth, no, nor at the sixth time neither.

– What did you do then?

– What! why, I could not tell what to do.

– Had you not thoughts of leaving off praying?

– Yes, and a hundred times twice told.

– And what was the reason you did not?

– I believed that it was true which had been told me, to wit, that without the righteousness of this Christ, all the world could not save me.... So I continued praying, until the Father showed me his Son.

– And how was he revealed unto you?

– I did not see him with my bodily eyes, but with the eyes of

mine understanding; and thus it was: one day I was very sad, I
think sadder than at any one time in my life; and this sadness
was through a fresh sight of the greatness and vileness of my
sins. And I was then looking for nothing but hell, and the ev-
erlasting damnation of my soul. Suddenly, as I thought, I saw
the Lord Jesus look down from heaven upon me, and saying,
'believe in the Lord Jesus Christ, and thou shalt be saved.'"

Now, whether this "revelation" has indeed been sent by
God or has been generated by the petitioner's own cornered
mind is difficult to ascertain, but it is clear that there is here no
objectivity and precious little disinterested search for reality. If
what is touted to us as "sacred" texts has been recorded under
similarly excited states of mind, their reliability as God's message is nil; as is the reliability of contacts with God presumably
achieved by other evangelical third parties.

And so, the Truth of revelation that the pure in heart and
the poor in spirit so heavily rely upon is hardly reliable. We cannot be sure that it was indeed God who spoke to Moses, Paul,
and Mohammed hundreds of years ago. In fact, the probability
is rather low. It is most unlikely that God, if He wished to im-
part some information to mankind, would resort to the totally
unreliable mode of telling His thoughts to a single individual
who is to spread the news to others. Given that God can easily
arrange to speak directly to the entire population of the planet,
it is highly doubtful that He would choose a way of communication that would almost certainly cause His message to be
doubted, could easily corrupt it in transition, and just invites
easy fakery. Such a mode of revelation inevitably presents us
with a dilemma: is it indeed God speaking through a man, or
a man, in all sincerity, attributing the effusions of his own excited psyche to the intervention of God? Do we hear the word
of God, or the word of man? If we believe the message, are
we displaying faith in God or a trust in man? Such an uncer-

tain mode of revelation confuses us much more than it can possibly enlighten us. The revelation, to be reliably acceptable, needs to bypass the second party altogether. The First party – God – should talk directly to the public, like in the following scenario: Annually, God summons the whole of mankind to a "town hall meeting" and confirms that specific texts indeed contain His ultimate message to mankind. His speech is followed by a question-and-answer session and is witnessed with the cold objectivity of mankind's collective senses and is electronically recorded for future reference.

With this scenario in place, we would not have had the multitude of religions. Just as in science, where only one physics and only one chemistry are being maintained by lopping off the competing theories, however ingenious, that are not confirmed by experiment, so we could have kept religion in trim shape, and avoided the present-day multiplicity of religions. This scenario would allow us to stay in clear theological waters indeed, but, much to our regret, it does not presently occur. The deafening and deadly Babel of many Judaisms, profusion of Christianities, and multitude of Islams rules full sway over today's world of spirit.

THE FRUIT OF KNOWLEDGE

So, it turns out after all that the pure in heart and the poor in spirit valiantly fighting to impose God's will have made fools of themselves. Their claim to know the Truth is a fallacy. What they are confident of being True merely may be true. The events they assure us to have happened merely may have happened. Texts they claim to be the word of God merely may have been uttered by God. The person they venerate as the prophet merely may have been a prophet. The little "may be" makes all the difference in the world. To borrow Mark Twain's phrase, the difference between "true" and "may be true" is like the difference between a lightning and a lightning bug: what "may be true" may just as well be not true at all. The error of a Truth-trumpeting pure in heart is in fact very trivial. It is a simple logical error of equating possibility with certainty. It is that error, rather than some "evil" operating in those who kill to advance their Truth, that is ultimately responsible for most of the bloodshed we witness in the news and read in the history books.

Paradoxically, they are in error even if the texts they claim to have come from God, came from God indeed; they are in error even if the person they venerate as a prophet was, in fact, a prophet. The actual veracity of their Truth is simply irrelevant. The problem is not with the historical facts but with their claiming to know them. This knowledge is illegitimate. Moses could have, in fact, been a prophet and so could have Mohammed; Jesus could have been a son of God and a Savior of mankind; yet no one has a right to categorically say so. Doing so is an error, since the physical realities of our existence outlaw any statement of certainty in this matter.

The reason for their falling in error is as simple as the error itself. They erred because they forgot to include one critically important element into their spiritual picture: themselves. Instead of looking at the spiritual world from the point of view of finite beings with limited abilities that we are, the pure in heart operate in some amorphous, nebulously impersonal grand world of absolutes that has nothing to do with the reality in which we live.

They stretched their ability to know way too far, way over legitimately safe limits, and this is why they fell into the pitfall of error. Had they been contented with mere faith, nothing bad would have happened to them and the others. They would not have gone on a murderous rampage, and many would have kept their lives. The world "faith" itself seems to have been intended to keep us out of trouble. The word implies trust and hope, rather than certainty. Just by its very definition, the first and most fundamental article of faith is, "what is believed to be true, what is hoped to be true, is not necessarily true."

But faith is too weak a drink for mighty spiritual thirst of the pure-in-heart; nothing but Truth would serve. Where there is a demand, supply is not far off. Just stretch your hand and pluck. Take anything you wish, and call it Truth. Guard it, worship it, kill for it.

ADAM'S FALL – AND OURS

Amazingly, we have been many times forewarned against precisely this impetuous, headlong rush towards Truth that led the pure in heart. The old biblical story that contains this warning has been told to us over and over and over again, was heavily commented on by the Jews, was used for the very cornerstone of their religion by the Christians – but obviously to no effect at all. This is the story of the trap into which the first human couple fell, their fall having become the original Fall and having caused mankind innumerable troubles. The story describes the condition and fall of the pure in heart and poor in spirit so amazingly well that, much as it has been told and re-told, we cannot avoid retelling it here, yet one more time.

As the Bible tells us, Adam and Eve dwelled happily in the garden of Paradise, leading a pastoral existence of cultivating its exotic orchards. The earth was then imbibed with the living presence of God, and there was peace among all living creatures. There was no war, no strife to mar the universal bliss. God Himself was dwelling among His creatures, and was frequently seen as a person walking in the gardens of Earth and talking to the first human couple.

That idyll was ruptured with a suddenness that was star-tling. In a nick of time, one beast was tearing up the other; the pleasant, smiling skies started pouring hail, snow, and rain; Adam and Eve were relentlessly thrown out of their lovely abode to till hard soil in sweat and pain. God was no longer among them to talk to them and to instruct them, but had withdrawn from their presence and had became inaccessible.

There was a reason for such sudden and adverse change, for the original bliss was not unconditional. There were two trees growing amidst the Paradise: the Tree of Life and the Tree of Knowledge. The first human couple, while enjoying perfect freedom, had one single restriction put on them. God forbade them to eat the fruit of the Tree of Knowledge. At first they obeyed. But their curiosity grew, and finally it took over. They fell to temptation. They reached for the fruit of the interdicted Truth and ate of it, not heeding the explicit Divine prohibition. Misery ensued.

This is precisely the story of poor-in-heart and pure-in-spirit. Not content to allow God into their lives through faith, they expel Him through their lust for certainty and Truth, with the same miserable result. Both the first couple and their pos-terity use illegitimate methods to attain the Truth. The first couple seized the fruit from the tree of Knowledge to which they were not entitled by their Maker. So, in their own way, do the pure-in-heart and the poor-in-spirit. By confidently swal-lowing as the Truth what is not necessarily true, they engorge the forbidden fruit of Knowledge all over again. For the tree of knowledge ever stands amid us: given our innate ability to think, we cannot help it, but we ripen and hang a new fruit on it every time we come up with an interesting, plausible, appeal-ing new idea. While idea pertaining to the natural sciences can be proven (or proven to be wrong) by repeated and repeatable experiments and is therefore a legitimate mental diet, many others are either irrelevant or un-provable. "Torah is the word of God," "one can only be saved through Jesus," "Mohammed is the seal of prophets," "the victory of communism is inevitable," "Aryans are a higher race," all hang from the branches of that treacherous tree, tempting us with sweet guarantees of sure salvation, if not with godhead. And misery follows every time we set our hearts on them. Never had a greater piece of wisdom than the story of Adam and Eve been imparted to us; yet far from learning from the original fall of our first ancestors, we are trying to repair it with the other one, this time of our own.

DEFENDING THE UN-DEFENDABLE

If Adam and Eve did not fall! If we were content just with faith! Faith would have saved the world a lot of trouble, and a lot of pain and death. Truth-trumpeters just bristle with a desire for action, their nostrils distended, their eyes red, their mouths shouting, their muscles tense, fingers on the triggers. Hit, kill, defend the Truth! How different it would all have been had they only had faith! Not being Truth, faith does not prompt action, since the perceived will of God may not be God's will at all, since the alleged reward for "obedience to God" may be a mere figment of the imagination and not materialize at all. September 11th hijackers knew a couple of Truths: that God commanded expulsion of Americans from the Arabian peninsula, and that their suicidal acts would give them and their families admission to paradise, there to have sex with pure or "purified" virgins for ever and ever. Had they had faith, they would have known that neither part of their motivation was necessarily true. Realizing that Koran was not necessarily God's word, they would have known that God may well have no grudge against the Americans wherever they may be, no matter what the Koran or Hadith or mullahs or ayatollahs or imams say. They would have known that the reward for murder compounded by self-murder is not necessarily a paradise but quite possibly some other place; they would have known that paradise itself is perhaps not a bordello, however desirable such an arrangement is for a gent in an aroused condition.

False sense of knowing God's will gave them the confidence and motivation and energy to act; faith would have substituted this with humility. Had they had faith, they would have been much slower in disposing of the lives of others, as well as of their own, knowing full well that a bird in the hand was worth a dozen in the bush. The very uncertainty of spiritual truth when approached through faith removes the motivation to act, since we act only when we feel we have all the facts in hand to justify action. Knowledge empowers and propels action; faith discourages it, giving no certainty that one's proceedings are right and in line with God's will.

Grabbing at illegitimate Truth makes us not only quarrelsome and violent, but ridiculous too. There is no letting go; Truth must be defended, no matter how little sense it makes. One such instance comes to mind.

A rabbi once told me that all the Torah – in which he included the whole corpus of Jewish religious writings, including the books of the Old Testament with the commentaries, the Talmud, the prayers, the writings of prominent rabbis – was the precisely recorded word of God. I responded by telling him that I knew of at least one instance when that was manifestly untrue. One of the prayers recited during Jewish High holidays of the New Year and Yom Kippur (the Day of Atonement) runs approximately as follows: On the Jewish New Year the Almighty records the destiny of each person for the year to come. He records who will live through that year and who will die, who will become poor and who will become rich, who will perish by fire and who by water, etc. He seals that book of yearly fate ten days later, on Yom Kippur, making the divine decree for the coming year irrevocable. However, repentance and acts of charity in the ten-day period in between the holidays can alter the inauspicious decree. If that part of the Torah were true indeed, I argued, no one would ever be dying in the ten-day period between the Jewish New Year and Yom Kippur. In order to give us a chance God would have to wait the full ten days until Yom Kippur for the signs of repentance. A person's death, say, on the third day after the arrival of the New Year would not only deprive him of a chance to repent during the following seven days but, worse, it would mean that the Book of Fate for the forthcoming year has become sealed prematurely, a week before Yom Kippur. The annual ten-day period in which no one died would have been an observable phenomenon, conspicuously visible in statistics of mortality. Was it? I felt sure that this time I got him. But guess what? He stayed silent and would say nothing, and then simply restated that this prayer, too, was the word of God, as if I had never uttered a word. In his mind, probably, turning a deaf ear to the opponent was indeed the best way to defend the Truth.

Such a mechanism of defense is apparently widespread and is considered effective. This, at least, is my own experience.

Thus, a proselytizing evangelical gentleman once patiently listened to my criticism of Christian theology and honestly agreed that he was unable to object to it in a logical and rational fashion. That fact, however, did not ruffle his confidence. It did not cause him to doubt and re-examine his position. On the contrary, he remained completely unperturbed and, to show that he was far from being defeated, told me in response that he would pray for me. Another zealous pure-in-heart gentleman, after having had a similar conversation, became furious and, having pointed to his Bible shouted, "Will you tell God what to do?" and left me in a huff, while I tried to understand his reasons for being so confident in the divine authorship of the Bible. Incidentally, I could never get any of these people to clearly explain to me why they accept the Bible as the word of God. In a conversation, I suggested to them that, according to their logic – or the absence thereof – since they have accepted the Bible as the word of God just because it *was* the Word of God, they should have accepted the divine authorship of the Koran, too. They invariably refused to do that, however. They criticized the Koran. I, in turn, agreed with their criticism of the Koran and suggested that they look at the Bible with the same commendable impartiality with which they eyed the Koran, and apply their criticism of Koran to the Bible. Again they refused. To argue with them was useless. As Shakespeare put it when describing a king who got it into his head that his wife had been disloyal to him,

"You may as well forbid the sea for to obey the Moon,

As or by oath remove, or council shake

The fabric of his folly, whose foundation

Is piled upon his faith..."

My latest such encounter happened in London. I was walking through Hyde park and, on its corner, noticed a small crowd surrounding a tall and dignified-looking bearded gentleman who stood on the top rung of a small folding ladder. Attached to it was a large Israeli flag, and he was sandwiched in between the two hand-written posters, one saying something in Hebrew, another with words in English. The gentleman was admonishing the crowd to remember that God could only be reached through Jesus, that the Judgment was at hand and we better heed the message, etc., etc. The crowd jeered, and he roared back that he was not ashamed to look mad for the sake of God – or something of that kind, anyway. The gentleman seemed totally sane and I started feeling bad about people poking fun at him and laughing when he shouted at the top of his lungs. I intervened. I fully agreed that he might well be totally correct, I told him. But to help me in my own doubt, could he kindly tell me how he knew that all he was saying was true? No answer followed. Sensing the direction the conversation would take if continued, he resorted to the favorite weapon of defense of the pure-in-spirit. He simply ignored me. He would not compromise his confidence with the thought or doubt required in an intelligent argument; he would rather be jeered at.

TRUTH – OR IDOLATRY?

But being a laughing stock is not the worst that happens to the defender of the Truth. Let us ask ourselves the very same question that the gentleman from London disdained to answer: what are we relying on when we claim having knowledge of God's will? The answer is, that in the final analysis we rely on ourselves, be it our logic or instinct or hunch or dreams or wishes. An acquaintance once told me that he accepted Christianity because someone with shelves upon shelves of books and three doctorates told him it was the Truth, and having but few books and no college degree, he was not in a position to object. Yet, even in this case the responsibility for decision rests not with the holder of three doctorates, but with this acquaintance of mine who, out of awe, decided that the learned gentleman should be trusted. No matter what, ultimately one decides for himself. There is no escaping, no shaking off of personal responsibility in this matter. Try to place responsibility upon the teacher, the prophet, the wife, the husband, the preacher, the scripture – responsibility still rests with you, since you and only you can decide that another's advice is good.

This has one very important consequence. Defenders of Truth rely upon themselves to ascertain God's will, to find out all about God – at least insofar as His intentions for mankind are concerned. By doing so, they project the image of God on their own mind, and proclaim this image to be the Truth. We have seen however, that activity of this kind is completely illegitimate. If their Truth is a historical one – like the miracles, for example – they are not in a position to reach it because time hides historic events past recovery. If it is a revealed Truth – they are not in a position to reach it, because they are third parties. So their very effort of building such a mental image of God is illegitimate, no matter how satisfactory the result.

Now, this illegitimate image making, doesn't it ring a bell? The defender of Truth uses mind and emotions to build an illegitimate image of a god to worship; does he differ in the least from a fellow who uses his hands towards the same objective? That other fellow is called an idolater; yet our defender of the Truth differs from him in no way other than the instrument and material in use – mind versus hands, thoughts versus wood. Perhaps God indeed looks the way the sculptor had made him look. Perhaps God indeed said what the Truth-defender says He said. Doesn't matter. There are no excuses for the actions of either image-maker. Both fellows are exactly the same: same self-assurance, same zeal, same inadequacy of tools in making the image of God, same stubborn persistence in making it, same illegitimacy of action.

The conclusion is as inescapable as it is simple. The pure-in-heart defender of Truth is an idolater; this is the depth of the pitfall prepared for one grabbing at forbidden Truth. Truth is the demarcation line that separates faith from idolatry. When belief is treated as truth, faith turns into idol-worship. To state with assurance that "Bible is the word of God," or that "Mohammed is a Prophet," is to commit idolatry.

The method of production of idols is hardly important. A Baal-worshipper could be – and must have been – as devoted, as pure in heart and as poor in spirit as is the most orthodox Jew, the most evangelical Christian, the most faithful Moslem of today. The Baal-worshipper was neither perverted nor stupid. He did not adore his idol knowing all the time that his worship was vain. He felt the call of the divine and did his best in responding to it. The Baal-worshipper, the Jew, the Christian, and the Moslem all share in warm feelings of attachment to the Divine, for all the difference of their creeds. They are just like gourmands who all like to eat deliciously, but disagree on what is delicious. They dislike each other's menus, but each is utterly devoted to the joys of gluttony. While one likes spices, another prefers what is bland. One likes Chinese food, another goes for Mexican. But no matter what is on the menu, the pleasures of smelling, tasting, chewing, swallowing, and drowsily digesting are the same. So are the resulting satiety and obesity.

The worshipper of idols of wood and stone may have been rather too poor in spirit, which accounted for the lack of sophistication in his doctrine and worship; in his simplicity he adored as god the work of his hands, while the more sophisticated Jews, Christians, and Moslems adore the product of their mind and emotions. But for all the difference between their idols, both Baal-worshippers and the Jews, Christians and Moslems worship man-made images with their whole heart and soul.

They all strive for higher Truth, and they all rely on their non-existent abilities to arrive at it. Idolatry is the ultimate, religious reliance upon a power that does not exist in reality.

And that is precisely what the "religious" do. By touting their theological picture as "Truth," by confidently accepting alleged revelations or speculative theories in the absence of a clearly verifiable revelation, they deny that they can err. But as we have seen, physical laws such as the passing of time, and communication problems like the problem of the third party, make it all but inevitable that making errors is the essential, organic part of the human condition. By arrogating God's ability to know, the "religious" worship nothing but their own selves. God, the Author of the immeasurable Universe of which we know so little, is easily explained, His purposes are neatly arranged and described and conveniently set within the frame of human mind and thought. A human picture of God substitutes God, filling up the spiritual horizon and crowding God completely out of the picture. Idolatry is triumphant.

CHAPTER 4

THE WAY OUT

THE TASTE OF IDOLATRY

Though idolatry is attractive due to the certainty and sense of purpose it grants to an idol-worshipper, it is not to be preferred as a mode of spiritual life, because this advantage of idolatry is more than offset by quite a few of its drawbacks. For one, the confidence it provides is based on self-deception. Nor does the idol-worship grant much peace since competing philosophies are an affront to the Truth of the idolater, and therefore an insult to him personally. Though we live in relatively civilized times – recent events make a more assertive statement unjustified – and should not be too afraid that the righteous annoyance with fellow-man's wrong modes of worship would spill out into violence as it did in times past, there is still a potential for tension. In fact, even in the most civilized places of the world, like Belgium or Ireland, there is a good deal of tension closely related to the Truth, since a particular Truth is often a part of one's "culture," to be defended as the greatest treasure against the melting-pot attitude of the majority.

When idolaters come to the helm of the state, as is the case of Iran with the ayatollahs, for example, they cause a wrong culture to be created. "Wrong culture" is not an expression that rings true on our multi-cultural ear; we value diversity and see cultures as being different, not "wrong." Yet the culture based on idolatry is actually a wrong one. Iranian ayatollahs claim that a Koran-based regime is divinely sanctioned – yet the problem of the third party denies them a right to make such claims. The whole culture they instituted, the culture in which individual rights of Iranian citizens are suppressed in favor of religion is based on an error, and hence it is literally wrong.

And idolatry tends to produce unpredictable, if not bizarre, results. A few years ago, a group of Californians discovered the Truth that the tail of Halley's comet hid an alien spaceship, and voluntary death was the only way of gaining passage. They could not miss the space-boat – the comet would reappear only in seventy-five years, so they took a ride – one hopes. What one is certain of, is that they committed group suicide.

An idol-worshipper can prove anything by claiming to be able to know the Truth: he can prove that oppressive political regimes are the only kind there ought to be, that suicide is good, that to kill is right. This ability of the idol-worshippers reminds me of an amusing mathematical trick I saw when I was a kid in the fifth grade. One day, our math teacher told us that she would show us something really interesting – she would prove to us that five was equal to six. We were understandably skeptical, yet in fifteen minutes the blackboard was covered with formulas, and lo and behold – five was equal to six all right! We checked and double-checked the equations – everything was correct. Then she revealed the trick. Smack in the middle of her proof, she slipped in a division by zero. In math, this is an illegitimate operation – and it allows one to prove anything one wishes to prove. So, in life, does the ability to know the divine Truth. Just as in math, one can prove anything using such non-existing "ability," and results of such "proofs" cover the full range of possibilities – from instances of greatest kindness, to the worst of atrocities. Both the saintly Mother Teresa and the sadistic Tomas da Torquemada are products of the same phenomenon. Members of Heaven's Gate or of David Koresh's group, at least, hurt no one but themselves; but as we have seen, all too often the drive to advance the putative Truth results in the deaths of others. Just as physics backfired by causing Challenger and Chernobyl disasters when we ignored its laws, ignoring the problem of the third party can produce a social tragedy when we forget to add, as it demands, a question mark to the identity of the author of our "scriptures." In their piety the idol-worshippers disregard the reality of their limited abilities, so why be surprised at the result? Why be amazed that the sweet fruit of religion produces bitter tastes of Crusades, Inquisition, burnings at the stake, oppressive regimes, or September the 11th?

So, while some may indeed prefer idol-worship, what should the others, who wish to stay out of it, do?

TRAP OF "IDENTITY"

One thing to dismiss right away is religiosity inspired not by the sense of wonder at the world we live in, not because of awareness of being alive, but for the sake of "culture," of "heritage," of "identity." To such people, religion is important because it constitutes the cultural framework of their existence, providing link with ancestry and community, and serves as a cornerstone of what they call their "identity." They may be quite meticulous in their observance, but that observance does not signify an interest in God. Because their observance stems from their desire to maintain cultural continuity rather than from genuine interest in God, they just "wag the dog," limiting their lives to a puppet show of maintaining "culture." There is a heavy price to pay for such voluntary exile from the rest of mankind and for prostituting God on the altar of "identity" – the price not necessarily having to do with the life to come. To refrain from dating an attractive person because of a fear of "intermarriage" is, for one example, a hell of a price to pay. To be afraid of even the thought of reading the scripture of another religion for fear of compromising the "identity" does not quite contribute to mutual understanding and reduction of tensions in the world. Barricading oneself against reality, carving out one's own little world of "identity" produced results that are both tragic and comical. Mr. Hitler created purely German science by purging out of physics the worthless and degenerate Jewish theory of relativity. Comrade Stalin, appalled at the encroachments upon the greatest-in-the-world Soviet biology by the decadent Western pseudo-science called genetics, rooted it out with a firm hand by shooting those academics who allowed themselves to become contaminated by the polluting influence of the West. Those interested in God should stay away from the temptation to insulate themselves from the rest of the world, they should make every effort to see the world in its entirety. "We expatriate ourselves to nationalize with the universe, " Herman Melville wrote about the nineteenth-century sailors. Those on a spiritual journey will fail unless they emulate Melville's heroes in this regard. As painful as the process of overcoming our "identity" through "nationalizing with the universe" is, doing so – and being unafraid to look at any and every aspect of reality – is a necessary step on the path to God.

For those who turn to religion in search of a critically important aspect of reality rather than to use it as a casting mould for "identity," the answer to the question of how to stay out of idolatry is fairly simple. We should look at the causes of idolatry and avoid behaviors that are conducive to it.

Know Your Limits

Idolaters forget that their abilities are limited; those who wish to avoid idol-worship, should view any spiritual situation through the lens of human limitations.

One way of doing that is to adopt faith, rather than to adhere to a religion. When reading the putative scripture, one must stay away from the temptation to infer its divine authorship from its appeal, something that happens quite often. Just because the passage in a book appeals to us does not at all mean that the book has been authored by God. It is indeed reasonable to expect that if God were to address us, He would express His ideas clearly and would put them into a magnificent literary form, so as to make them overwhelmingly appealing. A logically lucid document would indeed be more acceptable to the human mind and heart than a text which is clumsily composed and spiced with morally doubtful, if not downright repulsive, precepts. Yet, these are not sufficient as criteria of divine authorship. Good writing, when it does occur in the scriptures (which is gratifyingly often, though by no means always, the case) indicates the divinity of their authorship to the same degree as good writing in Shakespeare or Mark Twain or Milton is indicative of their prophethood. Nor does the spontaneity and effortlessness with which the alleged prophecies flow out of the mouths of their authors prove much. Such lack of effort seems to indicate that the words were composed outside of a prophet's mind and just placed right into it – by God, who else? However, quite a few authors work in this way. The well-known English mystical poet William Blake, author of some lucid short verse and, later in his life, of turgid, ponderous, rigmarole "prophecies," claimed that the latter were just forced on his mind in their entirety – repeating, in fact, Mohammed's experience, though with far lesser degree of acceptance of his prophetic claims by the public. John Milton, who was blind by the time he wrote his massive and magnificent epic "Paradise Lost," would for several years wake up every morning with a dozen lines of the most majestic poetry just sitting in his head, ready to be dictated to an amanuensis. Were Blake's or Milton's works the Word of God? Were the Bible and the Koran? We don't know. For all practical purposes, it was humans – the human second parties – who spoke out the words and put them on paper, and as third parties, there is no way for us to figure out who the first party was, or whether there was any first party to begin with. Divine authorship cannot be proven from inside the text; the evidence must come from the outside, from witnessing God narrating it, and our very nature as third parties blocks us from getting such evidence. Rather than feeling trepidation when opening the Bible or the Koran, it is good to remind oneself that the purpose of reading is to learn something good, and only what is good should be extracted for our use from the putative scriptures, as from any other book.

Likewise, it is not good to get too excited by flamboyant sermonizing. In fact, it would help a lot if preachers and missionaries reminded their audiences every fifteen minutes or so that their statements are not necessarily true – doing their listeners the same favor of full disclosure as tobacco companies do when they print the surgeon-general's warning on the outsides of cigarette packs. Generally, keeping a cool head when dealing with scripture is a vital principle to use.

SPIRIT, NOT DOGMA

Legitimate excitement comes when one delves into spirituality, moving yet farther away from religion. The difference between the two is their source of inspiration. The religious are inspired by dogma, by the petrified record of putative God's word, by someone else's words; a spiritual person looks around him – and sees the touch of God in whatever reaches his eye. What we see around us is not subject to the problem of the third party – we see it all with our own eyes, without a middleman of a "prophet." And there are wonderful things to see all around us. We live in a world of beauty, of flowers and stars, of mountains and lakes, of birds and trees. We witness miracles every moment of our lives; all we need is to doff the blinders of our routine to start noticing them. The thrill of seeing a beautiful tree is as acute as that of a miracle read in a "holy book;" but the latter is only an uncertain hearsay, while the former is a fresh, personal experience of witnessing God's presence in the world.

THE PERFECT ALIBI

It is also important not to be scared easily by the thunderous threats of retribution for wrong believing that may be thrown upon us in an eloquent flow of loud words. On the surface, such tirades may sound quite convincing. After all, a particular group of precepts – whether the Bible, or the Koran, or the testament, or something else we perhaps never even heard of may have been indeed narrated by God to some prophet. Who knows? There is always a chance. In this predicament, being a third party turns to our advantage, it becomes our shield and serves us as an alibi. It protects us from any liability for not following the Word of God – simply because there is no reliable way for us to tell what exactly the Word of God is. Even if we decline to follow the religion that is objectively correct, we are not at fault, just as we are not at fault when killing living creatures to satisfy our hunger. The most conscientious among us eat only vegetation, yet even this diet does not exempt one from killing – at least of fruit and vegetables. Eating rocks or sand would have allowed us to avoid killing altogether, but nice as we would love to be to everything that lives, we are physically unable to do it. Some actions are made impossible just by the nature of things, and this is an alibi both for our dietary habits and for the matters of religion. Just as we cannot be put on trial for not eating rocks, so we cannot be held accountable for not having followed the right religion, even if there is one. It is sometimes pointed out, as a clinching counter-argument, that such alibis won't help because God's logic is different from ours. Well, if such is the case indeed, if God indeed bestowed alien logic upon us at creation time, or if we acquired it later on our own, than there can be no communicating with Him at all, no falling in line with His will, Truth or no Truth, because it is precisely the shared logic that connects different individuals and allows for communication. If God's logic is different, the loudest, Truest idolatry is of no help either. A Christian living the Truth of saving faith and upon death being told by God that the Truth he followed in life was perfectly True indeed, would be somewhat surprised to be assigned to a place altogether different from what he expected, and much warmer too – just because God guided Himself in His judgment by a logic that is alien to man. A Moslem who in dutifully following the Truth of the Koran has gotten himself martyred and on meeting God is delighted to learn that Koran was indeed the Word of God, that it indeed promised many pure virgins for acts of martyrdom just like his, would probably have fits to discover himself assigned to hell, for the same reason of difference in logic. A difference in logic (something experienced in this life by those who have to deal with madmen) would cause a misunderstanding between God and man so fundamental as to be past bridging. Assuming that our logic is the same as that of God is the cornerstone of our approaches to Him, no matter what specific path, idolatrous or not, is taken.

Apart from giving us a perfect alibi, one other advantage of being a third party is that we need not be awed by different Truths, and can freely examine them without fear of retribution for impiety. When being critical of some Truth, we are under much lesser pressure than the second parties in similar situations. Second parties have to be exceptionally diplomatic, as indeed was the case with Abraham when he learned of God's decision to indiscriminately destroy all the inhabitants of the sinful cities of Sodom and Gomorra and tried to talk Him out of it. Abraham, and Moses at times, pleaded with God, using human logic while presumably directly confronting Him. We find ourselves in a less stressful situation when we dissect ideas whose authorship we can justly claim to be uncertain – simply because we are third parties. We have glanced at the history that was inspired by a few Truths – those of Judaism, Christianity, and Islam. In the next chapter we will look at these Truths, insofar as third parties can grasp the bare essentials of theology, and examine them in the context of broader religious ideas. As products of human spiritual experience, and driving forces behind much of history, they are of not inconsiderable interest.

All You Need Is Trust

Well, let us be optimistic and hope that God understands our logic; after all, He created us and knows us through-and-through. Having hope, and having trust, is the best we can do. In fact, our greatest spiritual problem is that we like to be in control; we need to be in the driver's seat. In our daily lives we often succeed in fulfilling this subconscious desire. But on a greater level, we have no control at all. We come to this world – we don't know why – and hardly know how or whence. We depart it against our will, not knowing whither. While here, we are bound by the physical laws we do not understand and are forced to accept. We are manifestly out of control, and the "Truth" is the prime means of regaining it. The idolater's Truth binds God to His "revealed" Will, puts Him in a box and gives us a clear road map to salvation that we can navigate. The Truth puts us in control, which is why we love it so dearly and cling to it so desperately. Well, the Truth is unreliable and treacherous, leading to idolatry. Perhaps, after all, it is best to let go of the steering wheel and let somebody else drive for a change, trusting him with taking directions. Perhaps if that somebody else is God, letting go of the wheel is the very best we can do indeed. Living decently with regards to the outside world and trusting in God's wisdom in disposing of our posthumous fate, may indeed be the best course in life to take.

CHAPTER 5

LOOKING WITHOUT AWE

ATHEISM AND THEISM

From the earliest times, men have tried to comprehend the meaning of the world and, in an attempt to explain it, have developed many different theologies. On the most basic level there are two fundamental ideas: theism and atheism. Theism holds that an Entity who had both the potency and the desire to do so, created the universe for a purpose. Atheism denies existence of such an Entity and sees reality as merely a collection of inanimate matter which transforms itself into different shapes and forms because of chemical and physical laws.

TOUGH THEORIES

Though both theories sound simple enough, their simplicity is deceptive. Each theory baffles the mind, yet both do so for the same simple reason. Our mind is capable of manipulating only the ideas that have clearly defined boundaries. Both theism and atheism, however, cannot avoid dealing with an extremely vague concept of eternity, be it an eternal mind in the case of theism, or the eternal matter of atheism. As we try to find some fixed starting point for our thinking, we discover that it keeps sliding back in time without giving us an opportunity to get a hold of it. By our nature, we are unable to think without starting at the beginning, whereas a "beginning" in the case of such a global inquiry simply does not exist. Both the idea of eternal atoms or energies and that of a Master Mind deliberately creating the Universe turn out to be ungraspable. The concept of eternity defies the very terms by which we comprehend things. Its intangible veil completely hides from us the beginning of things; moreover, it renders the very idea of a "beginning" absurd. Because eternity is completely unimaginable, both atheism and theism are, then, equally perplexing to the human mind. Not only is it impossible for us to directly prove or disprove either of them; it is impossible even to fully comprehend them. Unequipped for a frontal attack and for definitive resolution of this problem, we have no other choice than to be content merely with the developing of our personal, partisan loyalties.

A Sensible Test

Just as in the case of conflicting theories in science, our loyalties are to be based on a degree of satisfaction with the way each theory explains some relevant phenomena. The phenomenon against which theism and atheism have always been tested is, of course, the fact of our own existence.

The explanation advanced by theism is extremely simple. According to a theistic approach, life is a miracle produced by the same One who created the Universe. Atheists, on the other hand, believe that life is just the result of a fortunate combination of atoms, achieved through the chemical transformation of lifeless molecules. Both explanations have their difficulties, which we will presently examine.

Problems of Theism

Our greatest problem in dealing with the theistic hypothesis is our innate inability to comprehend the idea of a miracle. A miracle means creation out of nothing, and we are clearly incapable of doing that. We cannot generate matter, just as we cannot generate knowledge. Our experience is, that to make one object, we need to transform some other ones. In our daily life's experience, nothing really gets created. A painter, though flatteringly called a "creator," does not create anything at all. The paints bought from the art supply store in tubes and bottles have been spread over a surface of paper or canvas. That is all. We are producing gasoline, and telephones, and electricity, and what not, but we do not, and can not create anything. We simply find a way to transform some pre-existing objects into new ones. Our experience teaches us that all things are created by a particular process, through a particular "technology" as it were, through a sequence of steps. That experience makes it very hard for us to acknowledge, as theism demands, that things could have come into existence all at once without any "mechanics," without any process, simply because someone wished them to exist. When we see an object and wonder how it came into being, we mentally take it apart and analyze its origin. We do that by some innate instinct; that is the only way for us to think. The logic of theism, however, demands exactly the opposite. No assembling of the objects or taking them apart, mental or otherwise, is valid. Theism presupposes a world where analysis is not applicable. That world is so completely alien to our whole life experience that understandably we have great difficulties in dealing with it.

Theism, thus, simply places the solution to where we cannot possibly gain access. Though the solution exists, our very nature makes it impossible for us to adequately understand it. Our bewilderment with the claims of religion is very similar to the bewilderment we experience when being told about some mathematical abstractions. Mathematicians can talk of the fourth spatial dimension, for example. Even if the fourth dimension actually does exist, we are totally incapable of visualizing it. We have no problem with imagining the one-dimensional space of a single line or the two-dimensional space of a flat surface; we are perfectly comfortable with our own three-dimensional space of length, breadth, and height; but we are unable to take one step further and imagine a four-dimensional space. Similarly, we know how to perform the task of turning flour, butter, eggs, and sugar into a cake, and the average person can bake it. We know that it is possible to produce a masterpiece of art, though we ourselves may not possess the incredible skill such work demands. But that is our limit. We cannot go further. We cannot work a miracle, nor can we comprehend it. We can only intellectually acknowledge that, if there is a person who can work miracles, nothing is impossible for him. Creation of matter, creation of innumerable galaxies, creation of animals and of man would not be a problem.

Atheist's Solution

While difficulties with accepting theological schema are intellectual, the problems facing us when confronting atheism are altogether different in nature. With one exception, atheism always moves strictly along the lines of a familiar, human way of thinking, and that immediately gives it a good head start in our sympathies. The exception, which we have mentioned above, is the necessity to acknowledge the existence of eternal matter or of eternal energies, positive and negative, as the latest big bang cosmology demands. Eternal matter or energy is something that is as impossible to comprehend as it is impossible to comprehend God. That seems to be the only real inconsistency in atheism's total reliance upon the adequacy of our common experience. This inconsistency means that atheism has to rely on two platforms, on both what can be comprehended, taken apart and analyzed, as well as on what can't be, while theism is more uniform and relies only on the latter. In any event, once we are past that point, the message of atheism is very easy to grasp. Man developed naturally, atheism claims. He developed from inanimate matter, through a gradual process of evolution. First, a simple one-cell being appeared as a result of some fortuitous chemical reaction in the warm oceans of the primeval Earth. Of course, any living being, even the simplest cell, is a tremendously complex computer-like machine, whose function and physical make-up are recorded, computer-program-like, in a single long molecule called genetic code. That machine-being is capable of assimilating surrounding matter as food, and propagating and producing offspring by replicating its molecule of genetic code and building a duplicate of itself on that basis. The complexity of this first creature is such that no scientist knows even in the most general way of a chemical reaction that could have produced such a creature out of a bunch of chemicals. But, according to the atheistic viewpoint, that reaction fortuitously occurred some billions of years ago.

Once the first living being appeared, it started to propagate. Most often it created exact duplicates of itself, but sometimes the molecule which carried the genetic code got duplicated imperfectly, due to some environmental aberration, and the resulting creature became genetically different from its parent. If that difference helped it to survive, the new creature would also propagate, and change, or "mutate," in its own turn. Then, perhaps a billion years later, there was a quantum leap. One of the innumerable single-sell creatures by now populating Earth's oceans gave birth while swimming near some strong source of radiation, or perhaps while passing through some unusual chemical. That radiation or chemical confounded the position of atoms in the molecule containing the genetic code of the baby-creature, and most fortuitously, the baby-creature turned out to possess a structure that is drastically and wonderfully different from that of its parent one-cell creature. The child-creature has a multi-cell structure. Each constituent cell of that new creature is to perform its own specific function. One of its cells will digest food, and digest food only. Another will move our creature, and do only that, though not at its own volition but by the command of a third cell, which is to exercise overall control. A fourth cell is responsible only for procreation, and contains the overall genetic code of the creature. The creature's progeny, atheists tell us, will in turn mutate and become more and more complex, eventually turning into cats, trees, whales, eagles, germs, worms, poison-spitting snakes, butterflies, dogs, flowers, people, fish, kangaroos, grass, bees, crocodiles, elephants, and every other creature that lives on the face of the Earth.

In general, the whole picture sounds quite convincing. For all its general plausibility, let us look at it more in detail, from close-up, and consider it from the standpoint of the mode of design of a living creature.

THE MODE OF DESIGN

The term "mode of design" may need some explanation. Let us consider a simple analogy. A tall boulder, standing erect in a plain, may be used to determine the time of day by the length and direction of its shadow. We may say that it is a natural clock. But how about another clock – a modern chronometer that is made of hundreds of variously shaped parts, each of them interconnected and fitted together with great precision – which works only if each of them faultlessly performs its own individual limited function? Both things are clocks, since both can be used to determine the time of day; but their modes of design are completely different. The former clock consists of a single part which requires merely a specific and not very unusual shape to serve its purpose; the latter consists of many uniquely shaped and precisely crafted parts which need to perfectly fit together for the clock to work. The former can come into existence naturally; the latter, hardly.

In every respect, a human body is very similar to a chronometer; it is just far more complex. We are not just made of some uniform substance; on the contrary, the human body is an assemblage of distinctly constructed organs, each having its own specific function, each made of its own specific material, each having its own specific design, each mutually interconnected with the other, and all operating in strict co-ordination with one another. Bones are clearly different from eyes; lungs are completely different from the brain; bowels are absolutely different from the heart; ears are totally different from skin; blood is very different from teeth. Each and every one of these organs is extremely complex in its own design. An eye has a structure similar to the modern state-of-the-art auto focus camera. It has a lens that changes its size by itself until the object we are viewing is brought into focus. The eye is placed in a specially shaped socket of the skull so that it can move. Various special fluids flow in, out, and around the eye to insure its proper function. It is connected with the brain by a wire of nerves, so that it is the brain that gives us the sense of vision. Our two-eye vision guarantees a sense of depth and distance, which would otherwise be lacking. And so it goes with organ after organ. We have a number of different bones, made of hard bone tissue. Each of them is shaped in accordance with its specific function in the body, from the long stick of the femur to some tiny, intricately shaped and precisely curved bone in the cranium. All the bones are sewn together by strong and pliant threads of tendons into a skeleton; the skeleton is covered by muscles made of a material that can contract and expand, producing movement. The energy to move comes from food, which we macerate with teeth, placed in two opposite rows on our jaws that are positioned so that the food may easily be swallowed and passed for processing to distinctly specific organs of digestion, stomach and bowels. All biological processes need oxygen, which comes in through the nose into the lungs, another organ of distinctly specific function and construction, that has a design and complexity all its own. Lungs enrich blood with oxygen that circulates through the entire body. Oxygenated blood is sent to every organ of the body by pumping of the heart – which is, again, an organ with a unique function, construction, and materials – through the pipes of blood vessels that permeate every part of out body. Carbon dioxide that is produced when oxygen is used up, is sent back to the lungs to be exhaled, the whole process having a set order and rhythm. Blood gets filtered through highly specialized organs called kidneys, that extract from it the liquid matter unusable to the body, to be expelled from the body as urine. The whole of our body is covered with a special tissue of skin, which separates it from the surrounding environment. The act of procreation is of a level of complexity yet higher, because it not only requires specific organs, but organs that are divided between two different individuals of the opposite sex. The work of all these highly specialized and distinctly constructed organs is precisely coordinated through a network of nerves that sends signals to the organs to start their function or to pause. This picture is very roughly drawn; and, in fact, the work of the living body is poorly understood even by biologists and doctors, great advancements in biological sciences notwithstanding.

Each organ is connected to, and depends on, the others, and only the proper functioning of each of the organs insures the well being, if not the very existence, of the entire living organism. In summary, the living body is designed as an assemblage of mutually interconnected dissimilar parts. As any engineer will tell you, such a mode of design demands that all parts must be in place, properly fitted together and interconnected, before the whole may start to function. Let us see how the atheistic idea of a gradual natural development fits into such a mode of design.

As an illustration, we can look at the work of the heart. The beating heart does not work as a completely autonomous unit. Its function is to pump blood through vessels that permeate every organ of the body; without blood the heart is useless. It is logical to conclude that the heart must have developed by the time blood existed. If the mutation that caused the heart to appear had happened before the mutation that produced blood, the heart would be a totally useless organ. Moreover, it would not have been able to function, because it is blood that gives it energy to pump. If the opposite had happened, blood appearing with no heart to pump it, with no blood vessels to contain it, with no nerves to control its circulation, it would have been useless too. Worse, in such a stagnant state, it would most likely be lethally harmful to the body. On the other hand, blood is useless unless it is enriched by oxygen and basic nutrients and circulated through the body; thus, the lungs and stomach must have already existed when blood had first developed, since it is the work of these organs that gives nutritious virtue to blood. However, blood itself is a vital part of each of those organs and they cannot exist without it: without the energy transmitted by the blood, the heart would not be able to pump, the stomach would not be able to digest, the lungs would not be able to inhale. Blood, heart – with all the arteries and veins it feeds – stomach, and lungs are so interdependent that they had to have emerged simultaneously. But given that the heart, blood, lungs, and digestive tract – and the nerves and brain which coordinate and control their functions – are all of completely distinct and dissimilar construction, and each of them is made of totally dissimilar materials, how probable is it that they each evolved in the same nick of time, ready and fit to assume their respective function in the organism, while each having developed through an accident-driven process of natural transformation? We are designed from dissimilar parts interconnected not in a merely hierarchical way, one organ just serving the other, but critically, in a network where the same organ is inextricably tied in a two-way function of both a customer of another organ and a supplier to it at the same time. Such design dooms any effort at picturing natural transformation, because essentially the whole being would have to emerge in a single mutation. In brief, changes that resulted in appearance of a human body had to be concurrent – in line with the theistic model – rather than consecutive, as claimed by the advocates of the theory of slow evolutionary change, of appearance of one organ, of one function, at a time. It is impossible that the heart appeared first, lungs next, blood some time later, stomach yet in a while, nerves in a century. Other examples of the indissoluble interconnectivity of distinctly constructed organs can easily be found – for example, bones would not be held together without tendons and would be useless without muscles. Slow, natural development is not a mechanism for producing something that can only exist as a properly interconnected assemblage of parts that are of unique construction, of highly specialized function, each made of distinct material. This must have been the reason why Charles Darwin advanced his famous theory of evolution only as an outline of a possible mechanism of diversification of a few God-created basic beings into the multitude of species, but did not attempt to picture the origin of life itself.

Well, perhaps Darwinism may work. Perhaps, a crow evolved from a nightingale or a horse from a donkey, when environmental conditions necessitated it, but how to explain atheism-mandated emergence of a vital organ like the heart, which can only exist in conjunction with other equally complex, but entirely different, organs? Even in the case of more autonomous organs that are less critical to the existence of an organism, one needs a good deal of credulity to picture the natural development at work. It would mean that a highly complex, multi-partitioned, specialized and highly useful organ just emerges in the right place and the rest of the organs obligingly move or change their shapes to give it room, and then connect to it. To use the example of an eye, and being as fair to the atheistic argument as one can be, the story of appearance of the eye would probably run as follows. As the first step, this extremely complex organ containing a self-adjusting lens and all of its other necessary parts has somehow appeared inside the head. It was then unusable, lens and all, being blocked from looking at the outside by the thick bone of the skull. Some generations later, there was a random change in placement of a few atoms in the genetic map, producing an opening in the skull, by a lucky chance precisely over the spot where the eye was sitting all this time, longing for light. Yet another obstacle remained: the skin was still completely covering the eye. Many generations later, the atoms of the genes got jolted a bit again, affecting the skin. This random change produced a slit in the skin, of all places on the body right where it needed to be the most – not on a finger, nor an ankle, nor a sole, nor the neck, but by a most lucky chance, precisely in the location of the center of the eye. This was a move in the right direction but, of itself, did not help much, because the skin was still covering the eye. Again, most luckily, however, the next random change to the genes occurred in an area controlling the development of muscles. This time, for a change, the muscle got implanted right into the surface of the skin. Which place on the skin is to benefit from this evolutionary change of the genetic code? Skin is the largest organ of the body, with plenty of room to implant a little muscle on. Firing as always at random, evolution found – again – the perfect spot, implanting the muscle right over the slit hiding the eyeball. Finally, the eye-lid covering the eye could be lifted. Well, not to much effect still: a special visual nerve is needed to connect the eye to the brain, and the brain needs to develop a special visual area before a creature could see. We were lucky in evolution's next few random touches on the molecules of genetic code. Both the nerve and the brain got, through a few purely random changes, modified precisely to give us a sensation of vision. And to crown the process, a chance twist of the genes produced a beautiful and useful line of hairs, just short enough and long enough to be perfect, to border both sides of the slit with the eye-lash. And then, the second eye appeared in a similar way.

Well, this is a good story with a happy ending, yet somehow I find it rather hard to believe. Let them who believe, do so; my supply of credulity is considerable, but it is not limitless. It may be hard to accept a miracle, but harder yet to accept the reality of such natural random transformations. And this was not the most difficult example to picture, nor one of the most typical, because the eye is a relatively autonomous organ. Evolutionary appearance of heavily interdependent and inter-linked organs like blood, heart, and lungs would be much harder to map out in any satisfactory manner.

TAKING SIDES

The devil is in the details, they say. And the details hardly favor atheistic approach in understanding the fact of our existence.

The presumably rational explanation provided by atheism, and the overall plausibility of the picture it paints break down when considered in detail. Apart from a strong intellect, atheism requires a great deal of credulity, too, and one has only so much of both to give. This is where one is to take a personal stance as to which explanation to prefer, atheism or theism. I, for one, do not see atheism work. I find it more rational to attribute our existence to a miracle, to a deliberate act of God.

Life is ubiquitous around us, and it is easy to get used to it and to forget what a miracle it is. We are such an organic part of this living planet that we take life for granted, and our daily routine and worries occupy us so much that most of the time we are hardly even aware of being alive. Yet, thank goodness, we do get vacations, we do get time out of the absorbing routine, and moments of leisure give us a chance to notice the marvelous complexity, harmony, and beauty of nature. When our routine is suspended, when we stop for a moment from being cogs in the machinery of the world, we can take a step back and witness the beauty of the world in things great and in things small. We suddenly become aware of a tree and a bird, of a flower and of a butterfly; and we realize that we live in sheer magic.

The conclusion is simple: whether our choice is to be based on intellectual or emotional considerations, theism appears a more sound approach to choose.

ONE GOD AND MANY GODS

There are two basic types of theistic theologies: monotheism, which claims the existence of only one God; and polytheism, according to which the world is a result of the activities of several warring or cooperating deities. Monotheism produces theologies that are somewhat monotonous and schematic, consisting usually of the Creation of the world and of mankind, of the Revelation of Creator to the creatures He created, of their final Judgment, resulting in bliss for the righteous and torture or annihilation for the wicked, and destruction of the Creation polluted by human sins. Theologies of polytheism are full of absorbing anecdotal details of rebellions and battles between gods, of their victories and defeats, of the humans assisting them in their tasks, of the gods taking sides in human disputes and fighting each other. Greek mythology and Tolkien's epics are most interesting to read.

Both theologies seem to be internally logical; but polytheistic belief is very seriously flawed. As polytheistic deities would have to coexist, each would have to consider in his actions the power, interest, and will of all the others. They would constantly have to balance and counter-balance their interests, very much like world powers do today on the global political stage. Each deity would be potent in its own way, but none would be omnipotent, since omnipotence is all-inclusive and would exclude the interests of the other gods. The potencies of the numerous gods would then be fundamentally impaired; none being omnipotent and able to act of his own will. A less than omnipotent being is hardly a god. Monotheism seems to make more sense.

Three religions are traditionally seen as monotheistic: Judaism, Christianity, and Islam. However, they are each infected with a doze of polytheism (more obviously, in the form of a dualistic vision of the world as the battle ground between two gods, God and the Devil, but there is a more important reason). Islam, for one, appears to be monotheistic in nothing but name, as we will see. We will consider these theologies (which sometimes include a good deal of history, too) one at a time.

JUDAISM

THE GREAT CONTRACT

Judaism, by far the oldest of the three religions, seems to have begun as a very simple creed and has undergone considerable changes during the course of history. The Bible relates how some four thousand years ago, God established a direct relationship with Abraham and promised that he would become the father of a great people, the Jews. It further narrates the history of the Jewish people, of their captivity in Egypt and of their exodus, and their journey to Canaan, the land God had promised to give to the descendants of Abraham. During the exodus, led by another extraordinary figure, Moses, Jews collectively accepted a covenant with God that would become the cornerstone of Jewish theology and overall worldview. On the surface, the Jews simply undertook to observe, in the most meticulous manner, a group of laws. These laws, brought by Moses from a meeting with God on Mount Sinai, partially regulated social life and partially pertained to the performance of sacrificial rituals. The underlying reason for the Law seems to have been, that the Jews were chosen by God to be His collective priests. The Law, both secular and sacred, was supposed to give them the purity needed to be able to perform their priestly functions, or at least to be worthy of being in God's presence, for He pronounced an intention to literally live among the Jews. Though but a little portion of the Law dealt with priestly purity, all of it, it seems, was aimed at purifying the Jews, irrespective of their social status or occupation, and making them presentable in the sight of God (apparently on a theory that like ourselves, God prefers decent people to have as neighbors, and would rather not live among thieves and murderers). The rest of Jewish religious history reflected not only the success or failure of the Jews in upholding this Covenant, but also the different interpretations given by them to the meaning of the Covenant itself.

The land promised to Abraham's posterity was already populated, and the Jews coming from Egypt had to fight, expel, or exterminate the natives before they were able to settle in it. However, they became culturally assimilated and constantly relapsed and abrogated their covenant when they worshipped local deities. God punished the Jews by military defeats and temporary losses of independence that caused them to periodically resume His worship. Their form of government altered, from the leadership of charismatic judges to the monarchies, but their allegiance to God was still very infirm. Quite often their own kings themselves became devoted worshippers of the local deities. At this point the Prophets came to lead the religious struggle. They preached two main themes. First of all, Jews are bound by their covenant to observe God's laws, and He will not tolerate their worship of local deities. As the prophet Jeremiah eloquently pleaded, "... My people have committed two evils; they have forsaken me the fountain of living waters, and hewed them out cisterns, broken cisterns, that can hold no water ... As the thief is ashamed when he is found, so is the house of Israel ashamed; they, their kings, their princes, and their priests, saying to a stock, Thou art my father; and to a stone, Thou hast brought me forth: for they have turned their back unto me, and not their face: but in the time of their trouble they will say, Arise, and save us. But where are thy gods that thou hast made thee? let them arise, if they can save thee in the time of thy trouble." The struggle for loyalty to God takes on a violent form, as when King Ahab kills every single priest and prophet of God he can lay his hands on, and Elijah revenges them in the impressive scene of his contest with the four hundred and fifty prophets of Baal. To prove them wrong, he suggests to test the respective powers of God and of Baal by their ability to consume a sacrificial offering. Elijah sarcastically advises them in their difficulty to "cry aloud: for he is a god; either he is talking, or he is pursuing, or he is in a journey, or peradventure he sleepeth, and must be awakened." When their prayers prove vain, and Elijah is successful, he kills all four hundred and fifty of them.

Apart from countering disloyalty to God, the prophets also harshly rebuked the merely formal observance of the letter of Mosaic Law.

SERVING THE ONLY GOD

In fact, the perception of the meaning of the covenant changed quite a bit since the times of Moses. Apparently, the initial idea that the purpose of observing the Law was to live in a way that is worthy of the presence of God, gave way to a very different interpretation. At some point, observance of the Law became perceived as serving God in a way of a servant serving a master. The new interpretation of the Law was simple, and superficially resembled the original covenant: God protected his tribe, and the tribe returned the favor by offering sacrifices and running certain errands, like waging wars with neighbors worshipping competing gods. This, of course, has nothing to do with monotheism. Monotheistic God is omnipotent and needs no one's favors. He may obtain or effect whatever He desires; it is simply impossible to be His "enemy" – for He has none to fear, having created all and being able to uncreate whom He chooses, and only a totally committed megalomaniac would dare to offer monotheistic God a helping hand. Offering to do a god a favor, helping a god to fight an enemy is possible only in a polytheistic framework of thought. Indeed, the potencies of polytheistic deities are limited, and they may well need to look for allies, even among mere humans. A monotheistic God, on the other hand, would have none of that. In fact, that is where monotheism differs in quality: it relegates humans into minding their own business.

FIRE OF THE PROPHETS

The prophets had an inkling of this. They felt that merely fulfilling the letter of the law in display of ostensible piety was not a satisfactory way to fulfill the covenant. If the intention of the Law was to have the Jews live clean lives and be worthy of the presence of God, rote observance was hardly the right way. Filled with the spirit of monotheism, they stressed ethics over ritual. To quote Isaiah, "To what purpose is the multitude of your sacrifices unto me? saith the Lord: and I delight not in the blood of bullocks, or of lambs, or of he goats... Bring no more vain oblations; incense is an abomination unto me; the new moons and sabbaths, the calling of assemblies, I cannot away with; it is iniquity, even the solemn meeting... And when you spread forth your hands, I will hide my eyes from you: yea, when ye make many prayers, I will not hear: your hands are full of blood. Wash you, make you clean; put away the evil of your doings from before mine eyes; cease to do evil; learn to do well; seek judgment, relieve the oppressed, judge the fatherless, plead for the widow..." The prophets also tried to break the perception of God as just the tribal protector of the Jews. In their view, though the Jews were lucky enough to have a special covenant with God and collectively serve as His priests, it did not at all mean that He only cared about the Jews or was only Jews' God. The writings of the prophets as preserved in the Bible give plenty of evidence that they felt God cared about the surrounding tribes, too. This was one implication of monotheism that they understood best. God to them was no longer the local deity of the Jews. He was the sole creator of the world, while the polytheistic deities of the local tribes were merely imaginary beings, worshipped in error. The influence of his Word was to be extended to other peoples, too. Jonah preaches repentance to the Assyrians; others anoint foreign kings.

But progressive as the prophet's ideas were, they did not ultimately triumph.

WATER OF THE RABBIS

It took another crushing defeat and Babylonian exile for those of the Jewish tribes that managed not to assimilate, to finally accept monotheism. But it was largely a pre-prophetic piebald monotheism of a master and servant kind; at least, it made the Jews avoid all contacts with the outside world. From the time of the Babylonian exile in the 6th century BC, ideological leadership comes into the hands of the rabbis, the experts in religious law. As their views on the function and interpretation of the Law of the Covenant became the official doctrine of the Jews, the universalistic ideas of the prophets suffered a permanent setback. In place of the unabashed, passionate, unfettered, and vigorous thinking of the prophets, the rabbis substituted the cautious, detailed, and pious study of the ancient texts, some of which antedated the prophets and had definite polytheistic undertones. To them, the Jews were supposed to observe the Mosaic laws because in that way, they served God, impossible as it appears in monotheistic framework of thought. The observation of the letter of the law became all-important. The law became "surrounded" as new and yet newer regulations, or *mitzvot*, were added to preserve its purity from contamination, to be later codified as the "Oral Law" in the Talmud. Strictly regulated observance became a hallmark of the Jews.

The Jews were out there to serve God; others, not having been chosen by God, mattered little in the great schema of things and were to be left to their own devices. Jews became totally self-absorbed. A nation with some great ideas to share with the whole world transformed itself into an exclusive caste of the Stewards of God, as tightly closed to outsiders as is the modern-day aristocracy. An interchange of views was but a poor idea. What could others offer to the Jews who had all they needed in the Torah? Why give the Torah to the others, when they were not chosen by God to receive it? Jews no longer took any active part in world history, and focused instead on fulfilling the high purpose of serving God through their observance, content, if not complacent, at being positioned so high in the order of things.

THE GREAT PERTURBATION

Yet the others, ignorant of the high mission of the Jews, did not choose to leave them alone, free to perform their sacred function. Some three hundred years after the Jews returned from Babylonian exile, the Promised land was conquered by the Greek army of Alexander the Great. After his death, his enormous empire split into several parts, each headed by a king. One of them, King Antioch Epiphanes, decided to enforce the Greek religion in every corner of his country, including the land of the Jews. Jewish rituals were forbidden. Neither sacrifices, nor kosher food, nor circumcision were allowed by the authorities. That was more than the Jews could bear. They rose under Judah Maccabee in 168 BCE and defeated the king. Judea became independent, but not for long. The country quickly came under the influence of Rome, and then Rome conquered it outright. The country was heavily taxed and rough-ridden. There was no hope of throwing off the yoke of Rome through armed rebellion. In fact, two such heroic attempts followed later: the so-called Jewish war of 70 CE, and the more powerful rebellion of Bar-Kochba, half a century later. Both rebellions were desperate and prolonged, but eventually both had been brutally suppressed and the country was drowned in blood. To prevent further uprisings, Romans exiled those who survived.

MESSIANIC HOPES

But before that final tragedy, Roman occupation caused religious feelings to run high. The country hoped to be delivered from oppression, but how? The mere force of arms was clearly not sufficient: Rome was a superpower with immense resources. Of course, the religious argued, the full might of Rome was but nothing compared to the might of God. The liberation was to come from God, not man. In fact, the situation was not altogether new. A thousand years before, at the times of Judges, Jews were often oppressed by neighboring states. That was happening to them for a single reason: they kept turning away from God and worshipping local deities. But whenever oppression became intolerable, they repented and returned to God. And God was not deaf to prayers of sincere repentance. He invariably sent a deliverer, who liberated His people from oppression. Thus, Ehud saved Israelites from Moab. Later, Gideon delivered Jews from Midian amidst God's signs and wonders. Then, Jephthah was inspired to redeem Israel from the hand of Ammonites. Samson worked prodigious deeds of valor against the Philistines. And as recently as some hundred years prior, Judah Maccabee defeated the armies of the King of Syria. If God provides the Deliverer, no one would be able to withstand him. But because the enemy's power was so formidable, the redeemer from oppressive Rome would have to be more than a mere human. The hope for the ultimate deliverer, or Messiah, was born.

But first, salvation was to be deserved. Sincere repentance was the key to throwing off the yoke of Rome. If not for the sins of neglecting the divine service, there would have been no Roman invasion in the first place. To deserve the salvation, the divine service needed to be performed with a new and rejuvenated spirit. Once the Jews realized this, the country became flooded with men preaching the necessity of coming to terms with God, of doing His will. Most of these preachers, who were upholding and stirring the mighty religious ferment that overtook the country, came from the two great schools of interpretation of the rabbinical Law, the schools of Hillel and Shammai. And one of the men who preached reconciliation with God was destined to become the centerpiece of a new religion. His name was Jesus of Nazareth.

CHRISTIANITY

JESUS: FIRST IMPRESSIONS

Little coherent information can be gathered about Jesus from his sayings, recorded in the Gospels at least a generation after his tragic death on the cross. To judge from the Gospels, Jesus had an unfortunate propensity for expressing himself in slogans rather than delivering a coherent and logically structured statement of his views. One thing about him is clear, however. Jesus must have been a man of moods, because many of his sayings are very contradictory. He could appear most kind-hearted as when he quoted Hillel's famous "...all things whatsoever ye would that men should do to you, do ye even so to them: for this is the law and the prophets," only to become most viciously mean just two minutes later: "Many will say to me in that day, Lord, Lord, have we not prophesied in thy name? and in thy name cast out devils? and in thy name done many wonderful works? And then will I profess unto them, I never knew you: depart from me, ye that work iniquity." He could preach love of one's neighbor but be haughtily scornful of the simplest and most humane traits: "another of his disciples said unto him, suffer me first to go and bury my father. But Jesus said unto him, Follow me; and let the dead bury their dead." He could be disgustingly selfish: "there came a woman having an alabaster box of ointment very precious; and she brake the box, and poured it on his head. And there were some that had indignation within themselves, and said, Why was this waste of ointment made? For it might have been sold for more than three hundred pence, and have been given to the poor. ...And Jesus said, Let her alone; why trouble ye her? ...For ye have the poor with you always, and whenever ye will ye may do them good: but me ye have not always." There is a Jesus for every weather. For all that, he became the first and most successful Messiah in history, to be followed in the messianic path by the less successful figures of Simeon Bar-Kochba a century later, Shabbatai Zevi in the seventeenth century, and David Koresh and the Lubavicher Rebbe in our own days.

PAUL AND JESUS

Such elevation of Jesus' status is due to the tireless energy, sustained effort, and unflagging dedication of a highly educated Jew by the name of Paul, who, paradoxically, never met Jesus personally but became Christianity's real founder.

In his time, a small group of followers of Jesus were trying to integrate their community into the larger Jewish society. At first, opposing the new sect, Paul appointed himself the task of wiping out their heresy and had been doing quite well in this endeavor. But one day, when he rode to Damascus in order to capture and arrest some of the members of that hateful dissenting group, he underwent a strange mystical experience. He was thrown off his horse, saw a blinding light shining in the sky, and heard a heavenly voice. Paul recognized it as the voice of Jesus. The voice asked Paul why he was persecuting Jesus' followers, and Paul was so overwhelmed that he had nothing to say. Maybe there was nothing to say, Paul being so sure that his Truth was True that he never even stopped to think, and therefore had no rational answer. In any event, after that experience, Jesus became the center of Paul's thought. Not only did Paul join the ranks of those whom he had been so eagerly oppressing; not only did he go so far as to preach the divinity of Jesus to non-Jews (something his new comrades, who were still quite orthodox in most ways, were vehemently opposed to; Jesus himself, from what we know from the Gospels, would have been righteously disgusted by Paul's "throwing of bread to the dogs"), but he made Jesus the very cornerstone of the Christian theology he developed.

True to the overall bent of Judaism, Paul focused his effort on understanding the central point of Jewish religious life, the issue of being worthy of the presence of God amongst the Jews. The very purpose of the Law of the Covenant was to enable the Jews to become a "nation of priests," to be clean enough in the eyes of God to deserve His dwelling among them, and they managed by meticulous observance of the Law. Paul, knowing from his own mystical experience that Jesus must have played some vital, messianic part in the schema of things, re-thought the whole problem of ritual cleanness in order to include Jesus in the picture.

THE ORIGINAL SIN

Being a person of very systematic mind, Paul started with a key question: why is there a problem in the first place? Why can't God accept man as he is? Why is there the need for the Law to make a man admissible into the presence of the Holy One? The problem, he decided, started with the fall of Adam and Eve. After the Fall man has become intrinsically sinful, and the sin renders completely impossible any link between God and man. The sin must be washed off before a man can hope to come into the presence of God. Observing Law, especially with regards to sacrifices, was a way for the Jews to continuously remove the sin. But Jesus provided a new and better way of cleaning off the sin by becoming an ultimate sacrifice. He made the Law obsolete and established the new covenant with the faithful. Sin must be paid for, says Paul, and the payment was made by Jesus when he suffered on the cross. To be saved, a man must acknowledge Jesus as the Savior. Sin will then be washed away by the blood of Jesus, and that person will stand cleansed before God. ("... they are all under sin,... there is none righteous, ... for all have sinned, and come short of the glory of God; being justified freely by his grace through the redemption that is in Christ Jesus whom God hath set forth to be a propitiation through faith in his blood... Therefore we conclude that a man is justified by faith without the deeds of law.") This method of coming to God transcends the boundaries of the old Covenant. Jew or not Jew, all were now acceptable to God through the faith in Jesus, and could enter the world to come.

THE WORLD TO COME

The world to come was a relatively new idea at the time; Jews, promised by the Covenant God's presence among them in this life, evinced but little interest in the idea of posthumous life until close to the time of Jesus. There is a good deal of evidence to suggest that many Jews hardly believed in the life to come at all, seeing but little point in it. Jesus, however, not finding much receptivity to his ideas among the Jews (who mattered the most for him, being of his own caste of the "chosen") and being faced with necessity to explain the apparent failure of his mission, explained away the lack of following by proclaiming that his kingdom was not of this world, but of the world to come. Moreover, according to him the end of the world as we know it, and arrival of the world to come, was to happen very soon. Incidentally, this focus on the speedily-arriving world to come produced an interesting effect on Paul and other early Christians: almost total absence of interest in developing a political theory to help guide the faithful on this side of the great divide. Interesting as Paul's theological thinking is, he is laughable as a political thinker.

SOME STRUCTURAL FLAWS

One aspect of Paul's theology is very impressive. He created a truly intellectual and highly sophisticated theology, almost scientific in its method. Paul saw beautiful symmetry in the history of mankind. By the act of one man – Adam – mankind came to be separated from God. By the act of another man – Jesus – mankind was reunited with God. Paul begins with a single assumption which seems obvious to him, and proceeds to construct from this a stately theological building in which God and man are mutually interconnected, with Jesus as a link and central joining point. Though an impressive and, possibly, internally logical intellectual structure (although it seems odd that redemption will come so late in history that millions of people will be left without even a fair chance of salvation), it has a fatal flaw: it does not square with the contents of the Old testament and the known facts of Jesus' life.

First, it must be noted that Paul's assumption that man is completely separated from God by original sin directly contradicts the whole of the Old Testament, a crucially important document for Paul, as it accounts the original sin of disobedience committed by Adam and Eve, from whom, according to Paul, we all have inherited it. The Old Testament presents the history of mankind as a story of God's constant involvement in human affairs both on a personal and a national level. As God is guiding, instructing, and chastising mankind, mortals like Noah, Abraham, Moses, Elijah, Samuel – and many others, both Jews and non-Jews, both observant and not – come into direct contact with Him, or at least come to His notice. Such involvement would have been impossible if the humans were as utterly obnoxious to God as Paul would have us believe. But the fact that the starting point of Paul's theology is very forced is only the first of many problems with his theory. Major inconsistencies become apparent when we compare what Jesus should have done according to Paul's theory to what he had done according to the historical record of his life related in the Gospels. There are tremendous and glaring discrepancies. The Jesus of the Gospels (who, let us remember, Paul never knew personally) simply has nothing to do with the ideal protagonist of Paul's theology.

JESUS OF THE GOSPELS

As we learn from the Gospels, Jesus was an itinerant preacher who shared a message and fate with many martyrs who came before him. A rather strict observer of the Jewish Law, he interpreted it from the prophetic standpoint, and passionately preached the spirit of the religious law over the letter. He dared not only to publicly propound such interpretations but also to act on them. At a time when rabbinical emphasis on strictest observance of the letter of the law had already taken deep root, his behavior was considered to be heretical and, more than that, treasonous. We must not forget that for the rabbis, observance was a way of giving to God the service due to Him by the covenant, and no deviation was to be tolerated. Jesus had the misfortune to be born about seven hundred years after the era of the prophets, whose preaching preceded his. The religious establishment refused to accept ideas which Jesus thought so manifestly obvious, and this refusal clearly affected his mental health and brought him to the very verge of paranoia. Quite understandably, his discovery that the religious establishment was completely blind to authentic religious values made him contemptuous of the rabbis. He himself, naturally, rose quite high in his own esteem; so high, indeed, that in his self-aggrandizement he started believing himself a god, in a rank of the Son of God. As he did not keep his views to himself but, dangerously, propounded them explicitly, it is hardly surprising that, in a time when free-thinking was a crime, he inevitably came to have problems with the authorities. Accused and convicted of blasphemy, he was sentenced to death and executed by crucifixion.

FORGIVENESS, REDEMPTION, SACRIFICE

This was the Jesus who Paul, in his majestic theological construction, stripped of human traits, to make of him an abstract Redeemer. The central element of Paul's theology, as we have already seen, is the notion that Jesus has redeemed mankind from the stain of its original sin. The pioneers of this theory of redemption had been quite uncertain about how that redemption was actually accomplished. They chose to completely ignore the fact that Jesus had claimed for himself the authority to directly forgive sins ("but that ye may know that the Son of man has power on earth to forgive sin"). An acceptance of that claim would have left Jesus' suffering on the cross theologically meaningless, because there would simply have been no need for Jesus' crucifixion if sins could be forgiven by his mere words. What then evolved were two distinctly different explanations, both focusing on his death. (Interestingly, both explanations contain a problem which is a reverse image of the one which cripples the theory of forgiveness: because they assign ultimate theological meaning and value to Jesus' death, those theories effectively remove any meaning from his earthly activities; Jesus' preaching and miracles become insignificant sidelines to his main role of redeeming mankind through his death.)

Peter, one of the original followers of Jesus, assumed that Jesus took upon himself the collective sins of mankind and redeemed them through his suffering ("[Jesus] his own self bare our sins in his own body on the tree.") However, the testimony of the Gospels flatly contradicts such assumption. One result of absorbing collective sin is suffering collective guilt. While there is no evidence that every person's conscience was relieved, as it should have been had Jesus somehow managed to transfer everyone's sin to himself, we do have evidence that Jesus' own conscience was not at all bothered by the guilt of numberless crimes he supposedly bore. Even without reading Dostoyevsky we know how a guilty conscience can torment a sensitive person, causing him to seek oblivion – sometimes in wine, sometimes in death. The Gospels describe the last hours of Jesus in great detail. We learn, among other things, that he asked God to forgive his executioners "because they don't know what they are doing." His words clearly imply that he thought himself innocent. If Peter were right, Jesus ought to have welcomed his approaching death; but his prayer was not to invite the "deadly cup," but to avert it. To this indirect evidence we can add a firm fact which completely negates Peter's Redemption theory: Jesus' resurrection. Resurrection flatly contradicts Jesus' attainment of redemption. Redemption is "payment in full," and the payment for sin, according to the New testament writings, is either the death or the eternal torture. If so, redemption of mankind with later resurrection is as impossible as "having your cake and eating it, too."

The facts as related in the New testament make it impossible to accept Peter's theory. Nevertheless, even if it is accepted, the theory poses more problems than it solves. First of all, the theory does not fit into the general structure of a theology of salvation through faith: it renders faith in Jesus unnecessary. Sins are absolved and paid for in a mechanical and summary way. Those "saved" are not even personally involved. Secondly, Jesus could not have absolved the not-yet-committed sins, thus only those sins which had been committed up to the time of "payment," or crucifixion, would have been absolved by Jesus. (Peter himself must have had no problem with this, as he believed, along with other Christians of Jesus' generation that the Last Day was at hand and that his generation was the last one to live on Earth: "and then shall appear the sign of the Son of man in heaven... And he shall send his angels with a great sound of a trumpet, and they shall gather his elect from the four winds... Verily I [Jesus] say unto you, This generation shall not pass, till all those things be fulfilled.") Paul must have realized that the Redemption Theory was fatally flawed and to rectify it he came up with his "Theory of Sacrifice."

In this theory Paul suggests that Jesus has redeemed mankind by offering himself as a sacrifice to God. ("God made him who had no sin to be a sin offering for us, so that in him we might become the righteousness of God"). This theory seems far better indeed. Because sacrifice is by its nature a very personal act, one of achieving union with God, it needs the faith of the participant to fulfill its purpose. In addition, the union achieved through sacrifice extends into the future, and creates hope for forgiveness of sins committed after the time of the sacrifice. Thus, had Jesus been a sacrifice, the Sacrifice Theory might have stabilized Christian theology. Unfortunately, Jesus' death could not have possibly been a sacrificial one. The very nature of a sacrifice as a solemn rite requires a proper frame of mind among all participants. It is not at all surprising that there existed an elaborate ritual for a sacrificial offering. Two parties, namely a priest and the person on whose behalf the sacrifice was being offered, were required to focus their thoughts on the significance of the moment. The object sacrificed – an animal or some other type of food to be eaten later on – served only as a symbol to help focus the mind. Human sacrifices were strictly forbidden and were referred to as "abominations" performed in the ancient times by barbarous heathen tribes. In the case of Jesus' execution, no sacrificial ritual had been (or could possibly have been) observed, and there had been no awareness on the part of those present that a sacrifice was being offered. Those present were witnessing the execution of a criminal, a common and, to many, entertaining sight at that time. Nor did Jesus think of himself as an object of sacrifice, or else he wouldn't have involved others in his death, but would have taken his own life. To reiterate, a sacrifice required a solemn frame of mind created and enhanced by the ritual. There had been nothing of the kind in the execution of Jesus. His was a violent and undeserved death, such as many had been both before and after his, but it was not a sacrificial death.

Paul's theory of the justification by faith also falls short on facts. If it is only through belief in Jesus that a man can be saved, then Jesus was under a moral obligation (like that which drives modern Christians in their proselytizing efforts) to convince everyone of his mission, since whoever he failed to convince was destined for hell. Jesus seemed to have tried to convince his contemporaries of his divinity, but his miracles were apparently altogether too weak in their psychological effect to help him achieve his ideological purposes.

VAIN MIRACLES

Jesus' miracles (mainly healings and feedings,) were not directed to the eradication of miseries besetting mankind. He did not work them out of kindness, or to feed the hungry and heal the sick (as we know from his scornful "poor you will always have with you," he couldn't have cared less for the poor and the sick; if he did, wouldn't he have turned his miraculous powers to eradicating every virus and bacteria of every disease once and for all?) – but purely for personal propaganda. But somehow, his miracles, just like the ones worked by other spiritual leaders throughout history did not have the power to convince observers in the absolute superiority, less of divinity, of their author, which we naturally expect from such out-of-the-ordinary events.

In general, human attitude to miracles is one of the strangest known phenomena. According to the Roman historian Valerius Maximus, the vestal virgin Tuccia, having been accused of unchastity, had proved her innocence by carrying a sieve filled with water from the river Tiber all the way to the temple of the goddess Vesta without spilling one drop of water. The goddess Vesta had worked a notable miracle for her priestess, and yet, I do not know of any temple of Vesta in my neighborhood. A Lubavicher rabbi had told me how, just a few years ago, ten French women, who remained childless for years for all the visits to infertility specialists, wrote a collective letter to the Rebbe Menachem Mendel Shneerson, asking for his help. He wrote them back his blessing, and within a year each woman was nursing a baby. This was a far more notable miracle indeed, and yet, that Rebbe is considered more than an ordinary human mainly within a Brooklyn neighborhood twenty blocks square. Jesus and his followers encountered the very same strange attitude when they worked miracles in their own turn. One such reaction to an outright miracle is strikingly recorded in the Acts of the Apostles.

"Now Peter and John went up together into the temple at the hour of prayer, being the ninth hour. And a certain man, lame from his mother's womb was carried, ...who seeing Peter and John about to go into the temple asked an alms. And Peter, fastening his eyes upon him with John, said, Look on us. And he gave heed unto them, expecting to receive something of them. Then Peter said, Silver and gold have I none; but such as I have give I thee: in the name of Jesus Christ of Nazareth rise up and walk. And he took him by the right hand, and lifted him up: and immediately his feet and ankle bones received strength. And he leaping up stood, and walked, and entered with them into the temple, walking, and leaping, and praising God." Impressive as their miracle is, what follows is not the adoration of Peter and John as some superior beings with supernatural powers, whose message should be listened to in awe and obeyed immediately; on the contrary, what follows is their arrest by the authorities, who objected to Peter's and John's enthusiastic preaching of Jesus on the wave of their success. But the story goes on: "And it came to pass on the morrow, that their rulers, and elders, and scribes, and Annas the high priest, and Caiaphas, and John, and Alexander, and as many as were of the kindred of the high priest, were gathered together at Jerusalem. And when they had set them in the midst, they asked,

By what power, and by what name, have you done this? Then Peter, filled with the Holy Ghost, said unto them, Ye rulers of the people, and elders of Israel, if we this day be examined of the good deed done to the impotent man, by what means he is made whole; be it known unto ye all, and to all the people of Israel, that by the name of Jesus Christ of Nazareth, whom ye crucified, whom God raised from the dead, even by him doth this man stand here before you whole. This is the stone which was set at naught of you builders, which is become the head of the corner. Neither is there salvation in any other: for there is no other name under heaven given among men, whereby we must be saved." Of course, that gives the authorities a good deal to think about; and, naturally, we expect them to fall on their knees and acknowledge Jesus Christ of Nazareth as their Savior. "Now when they saw the boldness of Peter and John, and perceived that they were unlearned and ignorant men, they marveled; and they took knowledge of them, that they had been with Jesus. And beholding the man which was healed standing with them, they could say nothing against it. But when they had commanded them to go aside out of the council, they conferred among themselves, saying, What shall we do to those men? for that indeed a notable miracle hath been done by them is manifest to all them that dwell in Jerusalem; and we cannot deny it." It is coming, it is coming! Their hearts are on fire, their hands are trembling, they are about to see the Truth! "But that it spread no further among the people, let us straitly threaten them, that they speak henceforth to no man in this name. And they called them, and commanded them not to speak at all, nor teach in the name of Jesus." This sizes up the value of a miracle.

Strangely, Jesus could not or would not perform in public some of the impressive miracles that he had performed either in solitude or in the presence of his small group of disciples.

His transfiguration, in which he appeared, shining, in the company of Moses and Elijah, who were apparently paying him homage, would have made, one can be sure, a considerable impression on the public. However, it occurred in the presence of just two of his disciples. The resurrection could have become a truly impressive and memorable event, but had no human witnesses to it at all. Jesus' success in convincing the wider population of his divinity and mission was so negligibly small that it cannot be described other than as a complete failure, and totally unexplainable by Paul's theory of divinity and messianity of Jesus.

ANDERSEN'S TAILORS

The fact that "though he had done so many miracles before them, yet they believed not in him," must have puzzled Jesus and his followers a good deal, but they seem to have found a way to avoid doubt. "But ye believe not, because ye are not of my sheep," Jesus assures us, according to the gospel of John; "no man can come unto me, except it were given unto him of my [God the] Father." Thus, their solution is extremely simple: if you cannot break disbelief, make it legal. Those who do not believe are simply not supposed to. Nothing is wrong with the message, nothing is wrong with the messenger; the fault is in the non-believer. His Creator has deliberately made him incapable of absorbing the higher Truth. "Ye are dull of hearing," says Paul. Paul himself, of course, is absolutely articulate. It is those who do not understand him who are at fault. The whole subterfuge immediately brings to mind Andersen's story of the tailors who had undertaken to make a miraculous dress for the king, visible only to persons of Wisdom; who does not see it, is a fool. We should not take it too seriously.

John, Paul, and the rest of Jesus' followers must not have

taken it too seriously either, or else they would have easily seen that, if a predestination schema were true, Jesus has to fall out of the theological picture altogether. Proponents of Christianity assure us that since God is completely alienated by man's innately sinful nature, this alienation causes the need for Jesus as a mediator. But the very act of predestination is God's contact with an individual man. We are told that God took the trouble to mark some people as eligible for salvation. He had looked at them and contacted them before any intercession by Jesus, and completely outside of it. Predestination negates the most basic assumption of Paul's theology. Worse, if "no man can come unto Jesus, except it were given unto him of God the Father," than the way to God is completely blocked off. According to Paul, the Father can only be approached through the Son, yet John quotes Jesus as telling us that the Son can only be reached through the Father. This is a perfect theological catch-22.

All in all, Jesus simply has nothing to do with Paul's theories. Paul's theology has a place only among other unconfirmed, though admittedly ingenious, creations of the human mind.

ISLAM

Six centuries after the emergence of Christianity a new religion had come into being: Islam. It originated in the visions of Mohammed, a citizen of a rich trading city of Mecca. Highminded and deeply spiritual, he was in the habit of leaving the noise and bustle of the city for an hour of deep meditation. Once he was alarmed to discover some strange element in his thought, which, he was positive, had not been generated by his own mind. Gradually, he came to realize that he was hearing the voice of God ordaining him into prophethood. He started to preach in his own home town of Mecca, but the criticism of the ways of life of those in power imbedded in his message, angered many. However, many citizens of the oasis of Medina did take to his message, and invited Mohammed to emigrate. As Mohammed's position in Mecca became dangerously unsafe, he and his followers indeed moved to the more congenial and safe town of Medina. Gradually, Mohammed won many followers and founded one of the biggest religions the world has ever known. The words he heard were recorded in the holy book of Islam, the Koran.

As is evident from the repetitive rhythmic chant of the Koran, Islam was founded by a person acquainted with Judaism and Christianity both in their anecdotal and, to some degree, doctrinal dimensions. Contemporary, rabbinical Judaism seems to have had a huge influence upon the ideology and practical form of Islam, deeply impacting both its overall worldview and specific behaviors. Jewish dietary laws and holidays were widely imitated in Islam. Mohammed even mandated the celebration of the Jewish holiday of Yom Kippur, and adopted the Jewish custom of facing Jerusalem during prayers, until he had a spat with the Jews and modified both customs, to come up with present-day fasting on Ramadan and facing Mecca in prayer. The influence of Christianity upon Islam was superficial at best. Apparently, and not surprisingly, Mohammed knew very little of substance about it. Mohammed lived long before the invention of printing, and could communicate with others only through word of mouth. There was but a very small chance of his meeting in person a theologian of the class of St. Paul, to explain the highly sophisticated Christian theology to Mohammed. The only thing borrowed from Christianity is the obsessive concern for attaining life after death. The path to that goal, however, has been borrowed from the rabbinical Judaism and lies in fulfilling the servant function in the servant-and-master concept of relationship between a man and God. Basically, Islam extends the Jewish idea of coming to God through proper, prescribed behavior to all of mankind. In Islam, however, there is nothing subtle about this service. Throughout its history, Judaism oscillated between viewing the observance as some mystical and mysterious priestly function on one end of its theological spectrum and outright doing God a favor on the other. Islam, to judge by phrases like "if you help God, He will help you" scattered throughout the text of the Koran, heavily leans on the latter interpretation. Though Islam declares that there is only one God, and does so with a great deal of vehemence, it treats God in a strictly polytheistic way, as if He was not one, but one of many, and therefore in need of human allies. For all practical purposes, Islam is a polytheistic religion of a most basic kind.

The main concern of a Moslem is to get posthumous reward and avoid punishment. According to the Koran, a person must have a proper set of beliefs (most importantly, the belief in one God and in the Last Judgment), and must properly conduct his life. Among the obligations are prayer, pilgrimage, helping the poor, dealing fairly with one's neighbor, and fighting for the faith. In return, God grants posthumously to believers the eternal pleasures of paradise. Unbelievers and evildoers can expect to be roasted in hell. Both places are described with vividness reminiscent of Bosch's paintings. Hell is described with truly sadistic delight, tortures are described in detail, with gusto and gloating over the deserved fate of the unfaithful, who had been forewarned but refused to obey. The future delights of paradise are described with such delectation that the reader experiences a palpable thrill. The purpose of demonstrating such sharp contrasts between the two options of future life is, of course, to warn the reader that he had better believe. To use a briefer and milder example, "Surely those who disbelieve in Our signs – we shall certainly roast them at a

Fire; as often as their skins are fully burnt, We shall give them in exchange other skins, that they may taste the chastisement. Surely God is All-mighty, All-wise. And those that believe and do deeds of righteousness, them We shall admit to gardens underneath which rivers flow, therein dwelling for ever and ever; therein for them shall be spouses purified, and We shall admit them to a shelter of plenteous shade." With a message this clear and unequivocal, so threatening and so alluring at the same time, Mohammed must have expected that Islam would be quickly and universally accepted, but he was disappointed. Jews and Christians, who had their own strongly held views about the purposes of this life and the paths leading to the next, disagreed with Mohammed's "clear signs." That did not discourage him, and surprisingly he did not even lose his respect for the "People of the Book" – save for those in whom he sensed downright hypocrisy. But in others such stubbornness was puzzling to Mohammed, and to explain it without compromising the clarity of his "clear signs" and hurting his ego, he, just as Jesus and his followers six centuries before, came up with the face-saving predestinational explanation. These people must have simply not been considered for possible salvation by the "All-merciful," they were simply made to feed the fires of hell. "And those who cry lies to Our signs are deaf and dumb, dwelling in the shadows. Whomsoever God will, He leads astray, and whomsoever He will, He sets him on a straight path;" "Whomsoever God desires to guide, he expands his breast to Islam; whomsoever He desires to lead astray, He makes his breast narrow, tight as if he were climbing to heaven;" "God has set a seal on their heart, so they know not." Needless to say, neither the idea of predestination, (which implies that God is childishly delighted to play with us as with dolls, and has created this world as a mere puppet-show, amusing Himself by pulling us by the strings at His

whim), nor that of posthumous torture is particularly respect-
able. The theology of Islam is also problematic from another
perspective. The Koran exhorts us to believe in one God and
to behave well, to be charitable, to care for the community and
to expand the Faith – to do all that in order to merit Paradise
and escape Hell when it comes time for God's Judgment. It
is uncomfortably clear that God is given a rather pitiful role
in the whole schema of things. While man acts freely, does
whatever he feels is fitting; while he conquers the unfaithful
and explains to them the True Faith; while he establishes himself, marries, begets children, studies, and does deeds of charity – God merely follows and records every act of man so that
man may receive a proper reward. God is denied personality
and is reduced to a mere jurisdictional machine in the service
of mankind, busy mechanically recording all human action, re-
warding the righteous and punishing the wicked. Man, if not
quite more important than God, definitely has all the fun while
God has to busily keep on him His ireful eye. Quite in line with
its overall polytheistic approach, Islam seems to have a rather
overblown view of man.

Islam stresses the importance of particular behavioral
norms just as Judaism does and historically, it changed in pret-
ty much the same way as did Judaism. The rules of behavior
which were considered proper for a believer to follow, became
distilled from the Koran and from the record of the Prophet's own actions. The predominant custom of a locality was
also added as God-sanctioned. When all that was codified, the
general outline of proper behavior was turned into a set of
mandatory regulations, or Shariat, which is an Islamic code of
religious Law and is a close parallel, in form and in function,
of the Jewish Talmud. The mystical thought, exemplified in
Sufism, was later paralleled in Judaism by the Jewish interest in
Caballah and, especially, in Chassidism.

A PERSONAL THEOLOGY

THE LOGIC OF MONOTHEISM

Some years ago, because I could not accept any of the major existing theologies, I was prompted to attempt to construct one more sensible to me. To me personally, it still sounds quite reasonable and even convincing – which of course does not make it "correct," as I flattered myself by thinking at that time.

I reasoned that any theological theory has as its purpose the understanding of this world and our purpose in it, and that theology is in essence an attempt to answer a single question: why do we exist? That question logically transforms itself into, "why did God create us?"

An omnipotent God has no need to have us as His servants. Those who say that He created us to applaud and admire His works assume God to be vain and silly – a stupid assumption, to say the least. It follows, then, that we were not created for some selfish reason. We must have been created for our own sakes, with our existence as an end in itself. God must have created us in His Own image to give us a chance to see, feel, and understand – in other words, to exist – as He Himself does.

As we look at ourselves, we can see that we possess three distinct sensibilities which are possessed by no other living things. These are aesthetics, intellect, and morality. Aesthetic sensibility enables us to appreciate beauty; intellect allows us to analyze phenomena and to see connections among different aspects of the world; morality guides us in our dealings with other people. And when we use any of those sensibilities in a worthwhile way, we are rewarded with an uplifting and exalting feeling of accomplishment.

As our emotions are the most fundamental indicators of

our existence, God's image in us must mean that we have the potential to imitate God, to attain an emotional level similar to that experienced by God Himself.

God is the ultimate Creator. He creates out of nothing; we are given imagination, that cornerstone of creativity, which allows us to create worlds of our own through art, literature, and music, or to investigate the laws of Nature and put them to use, experiencing the divine ecstasy of creative achievement in the process. God is an unselfish Giver; we are given an ability to love so that we can feel the finest emotions in our love and friendship. It is by living God's emotions that we can come as close to Him as is humanly possible.

PROBLEM OF THEODICY

Of course, this theology has to address the problem of the existence of suffering, which challenges any theological theory. This problem, known as "theodicy," is an apparent contradiction between God's goodness and omnipotence on one hand, and the fact of human suffering on the other. God's goodness ensures benignity of His purpose toward mankind. His omnipotence provides a sure instrument of achieving that purpose. And yet   there is a considerable amount of misery in the world.

The Judeo-Christian theological tradition resolves that problem by transferring responsibility for the human condition from God to man himself, on the grounds that the first human couple had been subjected to a fair test of obedience to God but failed it and ruptured his blissful state of closeness to God and intimacy with Nature, justly deserving an existence accompanied by considerable misery.

That logic would have been perfectly satisfactory, but for a single crucial objection: God's omnipotence, and more precisely, its aspect of absolute knowledge, produces a side effect of "foreknowledge" which completely invalidates such explanation. God's ability to view future events renders the test itself completely unnecessary.

The "divine foreknowledge" is a major stumbling block for theodicy, and if it could be dispensed with without compromising any aspects of God's omnipotence (including His omniscience), the theological picture would be dramatically clarified. Interestingly, this is quite easy to do.

It goes without saying that understanding of any time-related phenomenon like foreknowledge is inseparable from understanding the phenomenon of time itself. At the present we do not appear to have a clear understanding of time, notwithstanding the theories advanced by both philosophers and physicists. Thus, our approach to the problem of "foreknowledge" can only be tentative. However, we can clearly outline alternatives presented by various models of time.

Traditionally, time is presented graphically as an endless line which extends from the "past" through the single point of the "present" and into the "future." It is this model that supports the ideas of foreknowledge and travel in time. However, we have a personal experience only of the "present," and cannot be sure of the nature of the other two components of time.

If the "past" and the "future" have actual physical reality – if, for example, they are composed of a row of physical locations containing encapsulated events – then "divine foreknowledge" must be a real endowment, though knowledge of what will anyway occur seems to be of somewhat doubtful utility.

However, it may well be that the world has been created in

such a way that the "past" and the "future" have no real existence at all, but are mere functions of the mind, which it uses
to logically sequence known and possible events, while events
can actually take place only in the "present." If this is true,
than the notions of "past" and "future" are similar to those
of "meridian" or "nation," which describe certain aspects of
real objects (like the location of a ship or a person's native language), but are not objects themselves. In that case, the notion
of "foreknowledge" becomes moot, and the question "does
God know the future?" is as meaningless as "does He see the
3000th floor of the Empire State Building?" If this is the nature of time, then our free will is absolute and in no way en-
cumbered. We are solely responsible for what we do. God has
no part in the existence of human misery which, then, results
directly from human actions, and which can be reduced only
by an alteration and improvement of our own behavior.

As I already said, this theory looks impeccable to me. But
for all its appeal, I have learned to acknowledge that its seem-
ing logical integrity does not necessarily mean that it is, indeed,
correct. It should still be looked at without any awe.

CHAPTER 6

A PIECE OF APOCRYPHA

A Sceptic Among Fans

"Blessed are the poor in spirit, for theirs is the kingdom of Heaven," a tall and strikingly handsome young man was telling the crowd. He was standing on the top of a hill, his long blond hair reaching to his shoulders, his calm face upturned, his blue eyes looking skyward, his right hand outstretched in elocutionary gesture. His voice seemed soft, but it was clear and strong. The people who gathered in front of him were looking at him with adoration. Everyone was quiet, and everyone tried to distill his precious words of wisdom. But in another second, there was a sudden movement in the crowd of attentively listening people. Someone was trying to get out of the crowd and was pushing the listeners aside. They let him pass, almost without noticing him, and looked up again at the handsome tall figure as if they were hypnotized. They stood oblivious to everything else. The person wishing to get out of the crowd of listeners was a short, muscular black-haired fellow, some sort of a craftsman or, maybe, a fisherman. He was mumbling something to himself as he was moving, but no one in the crowd paid any attention to what he was saying. Everyone was absorbed in listening to the glorious figure on the hilltop.

The short fellow was talking to himself in a rather irritated manner. "To think of it," – he was mumbling, – "to think of a fellow like that calling himself a teacher! And all those fellows around listening as if every word is a piece of gold which will be lost if they don't catch it! That guy a teacher! The guy who approves of the poor in spirit is a teacher! The guy who admires fellows who do not care to understand but are eager to follow is a teacher! The guy who talks in such solemn, wise-sounding manner, but whose words are as empty as the wind, is a teacher! Listen to him talk! Sounds as wise as if he were King Solomon himself, but where is the substance? Platitudes and commonplace stuff! Who are you listening to, guys? I will tell you what a teacher is. A teacher is the one who says: there is no such thing as the poor in spirit. The beauty of all wisdom is in its simplicity, and no mother's son is made such a fool as to mistake it when he hears it. That is why no real teacher shoots words over the heads of his pupils. A teacher, guys, wants you to understand what he has to say. He doesn't care to look important and wise. He just wants you to understand that which he understands, he wants you to know what he knows – and to know more than what he knows. A teacher wants you to be smarter than him, to be better than him. That is why a teacher tells you how he knows what he talks about, so that you can check it out for yourselves. A teacher talks in plain language, so that you can understand. And if you don't, he makes you ask questions, until you do understand. I'm telling you, the fellow who talks in wise, big words, which make much sound but little sense, just wants you to feel stupid, and to think that he is wise. Why would he want to do that? Precisely because he is not a teacher. A teacher cares for you. He likes you. He wants to make you better than you are now. He doesn't want to be awed, he wants to be liked. He doesn't want to be your God, he wants to be your friend. He is higher than you, but he does not want to stay higher. He wants you to be on his level, he wants you to be as good at it as he is, he wants you to be better than he is. But a fellow who just makes wind with his mouth is not like that. He wants to be above you. He wants your awe. He wants you to worship him. He needs you to feel stupid so that he can look smart. Then, guys, he can saddle you and ride you and you will be his followers and disciples and he will just carry along and feel fine.

"I'll tell you guys why you should not get confused about these wise-talking fellows. If you hold them in awe, if you worship them as gods, you'll do what they tell you to do. You'll think you are doing what God wants you to do, but you'll be doing what their dreams and visions and whisperings tell them God wants them to do. And if their dreams tell them "kill," you will kill. You will kill because you will know that the fellow who is great and wise and is next to God tells you it is right to kill. I'm telling you, you should be careful, or you will do what you should not have done and bring others and yourself into misery. Hear me out, guys: don't let yourselves feel stupid because that fellow atop the hill is so smart and uses such wise and big words, and pretends to be God-knows-who. You must realize that he, for all his fine looks and smart talk, is not any smarter than you are, not any greater, and not any closer to God. Then he is not going to ride you. Hear me out: just trust in God that he has not made you stupid, and you will save yourselves from killing. And you will save somebody else from killing you.

"Unless they show you how they know about God, and unless you see that their way of knowing Him is clear and fair, and there are no dreams and whisperings and such-like stuff involved, do not believe them when they say they know God. What can they know about God that you cannot know? What can we know of God anyway? We know that He is. What else do we know for sure? What do we know about Him that does not come from dreams, and visions, and whispering voices, and what one guy told the other guy that the third guy heard from the fourth guy? We know nothing, just nothing. Not a single fact that we can rely on. So why all that noise? We fret and fume like idol-worshippers, and to what purpose? What is the matter with us? Why don't we just own up that we know nothing, and simply live knowing that there is a God?"

But, as we know, no one heard him. His was the voice of one crying in the wilderness. Everyone was mesmerized by the tall glorious figure on the hilltop. Everyone was imbibing the Higher wisdom. The short black-haired fellow did not change history. History was being shaped by the startlingly handsome, tall figure on the top of the hill. Our bloody history moved on.

CHURCH AND STATE, TRUTH AND FAITH

But quite apart from all allegorical apocrypha, idolatry is a dangerous thing. While separation of church and state precludes state-sponsored excesses such as inquisition, it is powerless to prevent private expressions of violent enthusiasm, like the ones we witnessed on September 11th, 2001. As the weaponry becomes more powerful and more accessible, it is no longer the state alone that can inflict mass casualties; small groups of highly motivated private individuals are also becoming capable of mass murder. Today, more than a separation of church and state is needed; we must achieve a clear separation of religion and knowledge. Truth and faith should not be mixed together. In spiritual life, such mix-up leads to idol-worship; in social and political spheres, it results in oppression and spasms of violence.

The progress of human civilization will continue only so long as people respect the limitations which reality imposes on them. "Lo, this only have I found, that God hath made man upright; but they have thought out many inventions," observes Ecclesiastes with a palpable melancholy. The "inventions" he talks of are not the kind that help us to move faster, to see further or to learn better. "Inventions" are illusive human ideas. Illusions and delusions, when acted upon, bring disaster – either technological ones like Chernobyl or the spaceship Challenger, which happen when we overestimate our control of a situation, or social catastrophes which ensue when, in the eagerness to build a utopian society, people become frenzied, lose their minds, and pave the way to a bright future with corpses. Holy Inquisitors, Communists and Nazis were all idealists with dreams of human salvation. They had the very best of intentions. But they all fell into the deadly error of accepting as truth theories which, from a human perspective, could not be proven with certainty. They usurped God's right to know and, in their eagerness to impose divine justice upon those they deemed the perversely satanic enemies of mankind – the "heretics," the "rich," the "Jews" – they spilled rivers of blood, destroyed millions of innocent lives, and filled the Earth with indescribable and immeasurable suffering. But when their frenzy ebbed because they were finally defeated and brought to their senses, they discovered that their "knowledge" had degraded them lower than the beasts. The "true-faith" brand of idolatry is dangerously similar to the theorizing of those "saviors of mankind;" in fact, it has the very same roots of unjustified confidence. It is as dangerous because it is as intoxicating. It produces fanatics who find the only vent for their blind zeal in physical violence. To avoid future tragedies like those which fill many pages of human history, it is paramount that we stay in sync with reality and remember that it is simply not given us to know theological truth, and that we must restrict ourselves to what is possible to ascertain through the means we have been allowed, which are science and logic. To go beyond these is only to enthrone the Illusion. Illusory "truth" leads to discord and animosity among the diverse groups of "the faithful" who, emboldened and empowered by their self-assurance of possessing the ultimate knowledge, defend their doctrines, or try to impose them on others, or far worse yet, claim to serve one God with all the ardor of drunks. Let us not forget that the fruit from the forbidden Tree of Knowledge brought into the world only hatred and death. If the Biblical story of the Fall which resulted from willfully seizing the forbidden "knowledge" contains a lesson, it should above all teach us to acknowledge our limitations and to abandon fruitless and self-deceiving attempts to penetrate what is purposely hidden from us. We must learn to satisfy our thirst for faith with one single truth: that God indeed is.

SOURCES OF QUOTATIONS

Bible, The Old Testament – Genesis 18:25; Exodus 20:3-5; 22:18, 32:10-14, 26-29; 1st Kings 18:27; Ecclisiastes 7:29; Isaiah 1:11-17; Jeremiah 2:13, 26-28

Bible, The New Testament – Mathew 9:6; 19:12; 24:29-32; Luke 23:34; John 6:65; 10:26; 12:37; Romans 3:12, 21-25, 28; 2nd Corinthians 5:21; 1st Peter 2:24; Acts 3-4

The Koran, Translated by Arthur J. Arberry, Oxford University Press, chapters 4 ("Women") 55; 6 ("Cattle") 35, 125; 9 ("Repentance") 90; 47 ("Muhammad") 5

John Bunyan, The Pilgrim's Progress, 1838 ed., pp. 203-205

David Masson, The Life of John Milton, Reprint by Peter Smith, 1965 (originally published 1881), v. 1 p 60

Zoe Oldenbourg, Massacre at Montsegur; a history of Albigensian Crusade, N.Y. 1959, pp. 116, 141

E. E. Urbach, The Sages – their Concepts and Beliefs. Magnes Press, Hebrew University, Jerusalem, 1975, pp. 595-596

J. M. Buckley, The Midnight Sun, the Tzar and the Nihilist, Boston 1886, pp. 331-332

Wm. Shakespeare, The Winter's Tale, Act I, Sc. II, lines 426-429

Most of historical information comes from The Encyclopaedia of Religion, 16 volumes, edited by Mircea Eliade, Macmillan, 1987

INDEX